Voices of Experience

Higher Ed

Questions about the Purpose(s) of Colleges & Universities

Norm Denzin, Josef Progler, Joe L. Kincheloe, Shirley R. Steinberg
General Editors

Vol. 5

PETER LANG
New York • Washington, D.C./Baltimore • Bern
Frankfurt am Main • Berlin • Brussels • Vienna • Oxford

Voices of Experience

Reflections from a
Harvard Teaching Seminar

EDITED BY
Mary-Ann Winkelmes
and James Wilkinson

PETER LANG
New York • Washington, D.C./Baltimore • Bern
Frankfurt am Main • Berlin • Brussels • Vienna • Oxford

Library of Congress Cataloging-in-Publication Data

Voices of experience: reflections from a Harvard teaching
seminar / edited by Mary-Ann Winkelmes and James Wilkinson.
p. cm. — (Higher ed; vol. 5)
Includes bibliographical references and index.
1. College teaching. 2. Teacher-student relationships. 3. College teachers.
I. Winkelmes, Mary-Ann. II. Wilkinson, James D. III. Series.
LB2331 .V63   378.1′25—dc21   00-020593
ISBN 0-8204-4901-6
ISSN 1523-9551

Die Deutsche Bibliothek-CIP-Einheitsaufnahme

Voices of experience: reflections from a Harvard
teaching seminar / ed. by Mary-Ann Winkelmes and James Wilkinson.
–New York; Washington, D.C./Baltimore; Bern;
Frankfurt am Main; Berlin; Brussels; Vienna; Oxford: Lang.
(Higher ed; Vol. 5)
ISBN 0-8204-4901-6

Cover design by Dutton & Sherman Design

The paper in this book meets the guidelines for permanence and durability
of the Committee on Production Guidelines for Book Longevity
of the Council of Library Resources.

Printed in the United States of America

CONTENTS

Preface ix
James Wilkinson, Director,
Derek Bok Center for Teaching and Learning, Harvard University

Introduction xiii
Mary-Ann Winkelmes, Associate Director,
Derek Bok Center for Teaching and Learning, Harvard University

Teaching and Learning in the Classroom 1

Mastery vs. Memory: Conceptual Thinking
in Quantitative Science Classes 3
Rebecca J. Jackman, Post-doctoral Associate,
Massachusetts Institute of Technology

Lectures without Lecturing: An Interactive Discovery
of Key Ideas in Math and Science 13
Eric Towne, former Teaching Assistant,
Department of Mathematics, Harvard University

"Not in My Village": Reflections on Bringing
Musical Culture to the Diverse Classroom 23
Jennifer B. Kotilaine, Associate Secretary to Harvard University

Four Techniques that Bridge the Barriers
to Knowledge Sharing in the Classroom................................ 27
Leigh M. Weiss, Post-doctoral Research Fellow, Harvard Business School

When Good Teaching Techniques Stop Working 37
Jeffrey Marinacci, former Teaching Fellow,
Department of Sociology, Harvard University

Losing It and Getting It Back:
A Teacher's Basics for Leading Seminars 43
James R. Dawes, Junior Fellow, Harvard Society of Fellows

Overlooked Essentials for Classroom Discussions 49
Mary-Ann Winkelmes, Associate Director,
Derek Bok Center for Teaching and Learning

Teaching and Learning Beyond the Classroom 55

Getting the Most out of Weekly Assignments:
Using Feedback as a Motivational Tool 57
Sujay Rao, Teaching Fellow, Department of History, Harvard University

How to Improve Students' Writing Before Reading Any 65
Kerry Walk, Assistant Director, Harvard Writing Project,
and Senior Preceptor, Expository Writing Program, Harvard College

Making Grades Mean More and Less with Your Students........................ 75
Judith Richardson, Teaching Fellow,
History of American Civilization Program, Harvard University

Lessons from Michelangelo and Freud
on Teaching Quantitative Courses... 81
Todd Bodner, Post-doctoral Research Fellow, University of Illinois

Creating the Environment for Better Student-Teacher Conferences......... 87
Anne E. Fernald, Assistant Professor, Department of English, Purdue University

Notes... 93

Bibliography 99
   Overviews of Literature and Research on College
      and University Teaching   99
   Effective Techniques Recommended
      by Successful Teachers   100
   Teacher Motivation/Student Motivation   102
   Discussion in the Classroom   105
   Collaborative Learning   107
   Grading and Feedback on Students' Work   110
   Diversity and Communication   112
   Balancing Teaching and Professional Concerns   115
   Technology and Teaching   117
   Lecturing   119

List of Contributors 123

Index 127

PREFACE

JAMES WILKINSON

When asked to recall the most positive experiences in their education, many students name those moments when a teacher's interest and care inspired them to learn. One finding of Richard Light's second Harvard Assessment Seminars report (1992) was that "interactive relationships organized around academic work are vital" for those students who "get the most out of college, who grow the most academically, and who are happiest" (8, 6). Where do these "vital" interactions take place? Many occur in small groups—discussion sections, laboratory exercises, and tutorials—where teachers and students interact directly and repeatedly. Many of these small groups, in turn, are taught by graduate TAs or junior faculty.

What makes these learning venues particularly valuable as sites for "interactive relationships organized around academic work" is the conjunction between scholarship and interpersonal skills. Discussion leaders who succeed in creating a productive, stimulating academic atmosphere in their classrooms do so because they understand how to engage students both intellectually and emotionally. Thus junior members of the teaching community often confront teaching assignments where a mastery of process and group dynamics plays a vital role in the instructional outcome. For them in particular, subject knowledge is a necessary, but not a sufficient condition for good teaching.

In the end, most meet this challenge effectively—even with enthusiasm. But the learning curve is steep. Despite the efforts of teaching centers throughout the country and the guidance extended by many faculty to their graduate students as they begin to teach, the need for help persists. High turnover among teaching assistants and non-tenure-track junior faculty limits their ability to pass on the fruits of a completed apprenticeship to younger colleagues. The experience they have accumulated is thus lost for their fellow teachers.

When Mary-Ann Winkelmes approached me with a plan for a collection of essays by experienced teaching assistants, adjuncts, and lecturers, it seemed a welcome antidote to this loss of institutional memory. The contributors had first come together in a seminar program she developed; now they hoped to extend their discussions by reaching out to others in print. Writing about their teaching offered a way to provide other teachers with insights derived from actual classroom practice. The group members found that sharing these stories among themselves both improved their teaching skills and lowered their sense of isolation; what discussions had done for them, a written record of some of the points raised in those discussions could do for others.

"Voices of Experience" may seem an odd, even a presumptuous title for a collection of essays written by women and men many of whom are starting out on their careers. Yet in reality, it is entirely appropriate. As the reader will discover, these teachers have attained a high degree of teaching proficiency in a relatively short time. Forced to learn in a hurry, they have mobilized their attention and intelligence on mastering day-to-day pedagogical issues, with impressive results. The support offered by older colleagues and our teaching center may have speeded the process and made the transition from student to teacher less traumatic; but what gives these authors a distinctive voice is what they have learned through their own efforts, aided by the collective reflection of their peers. Because the learning process is still relatively recent, they write with immediacy and freshness of what they have experienced in the classroom.

For one element which characterizes these essays is their debt to what in anthropology would be called field work. In the best sense of the term, they are exercises in induction. The authors draw from their teaching, having gained a sense of what works and what does not. They present not only the raw material of experience, but also their reflections—the very sort of "processing" which we encourage our students to pursue in their own studies. The authors convey many useful observations, especially concerning teaching technique, but also analyses of why things work as they do. The British philosopher Alfred North Whitehead once defined education as acquiring "the art of the utilization of knowledge" (Whitehead, *The Aims of Education and Other Essays*, New York: The Free Press, 1957, p. 4). And for those who wish to utilize knowledge, there is no greater help than understanding the conditions required for success.

These "voices" are also inspirational. In a number of chapters, we encounter teachers facing situations that test their inventiveness and maturity, and succeeding well beyond the norm. It is important for all faculty, but especially for beginners, to understand the degree to which teaching involves constant problem-solving. Indeed, one reason that small group instruction is so demanding is precisely because the problems posed by the shifting interplay, among student personalities, intellect, and affect change continuously and dramatically. Beginning faculty and instructors can take comfort in the way these essays testify to the need for constant improvisation—a sort of pedagogical nimble-footedness which relies not on formulas, but rather on responsiveness to the immediate situation and sensitivity to class dynamics.

Finally, the definition of teaching and learning embodied in these essays is not one restricted to the classroom alone. As they make clear, teaching occurs in many locales and encompasses many activities. E-mail, office hours, comments on papers and other written work are all modes of communication which enable teaching and learning to advance outside the formal setting of classroom premises. A number of essays in this collection deal with teaching in this broader sense. They suggest the extent to which the intellectual stimulation that begins in a common space can be shaped for individual needs through instruction and comment outside the classroom.

Teaching can be an isolating experience. Beginners tend to feel that the problems they encounter result from inexperience or personal misjudgments, and would be more easily solved by a seasoned practitioner. When things go really well (as they can even at the start), there is often no one with whom to share this triumph. I sincerely hope that reading these accounts will help the reader to feel less isolated by demonstrating that the community of teachers is not bounded by time and space. The voices in this volume can speak to us in ways that offer both support and validation for our own private efforts. They can amplify the challenges and achievements that await us as we engage in this difficult but rewarding kind of teaching. Enjoy. And please, if you'd like to join the conversation, send us your thoughts.

INTRODUCTION

MARY-ANN WINKELMES

This book is a welcome if unexpected result of an experimental program undertaken at the Derek Bok Center for Teaching and Learning at Harvard University during the 1996–1997 academic year. The Senior Teaching Fellows' Program was designed to recognize the contributions of award-winning teachers who are post-doctoral instructors, lecturers, preceptors and advanced graduate-student teaching fellows in the university's Faculty of Arts and Sciences, and to pass on their knowledge about teaching and learning. Participants met regularly to discuss teaching practices and theories, challenges and strategies, and some of the literature on post-secondary teaching and learning. For these scholars in the humanities, sciences and social sciences, the program provided an opportunity to reflect on teaching and learning with their colleagues from other departments.

Together, the group considered cross-disciplinary pedagogical issues including students' and teachers' motivation, effective teaching techniques, discussion in the classroom, collaborative learning, grading and feedback on students' work, the difficulties of balancing the demands of teaching with other professional concerns like publishing and tenure, diversity and communication, and the impact of technology on education. The fellows addressed these issues with the same intellectual rigor they apply to research in their own disciplines. In their commitment to this scholarship of teaching, the fellows are representatives of a new generation of teaching scholars—a generation that grows as most academic departments enjoy the luxury of appointing new faculty who have distinguished themselves not only as scholars but also as accomplished and dedicated teachers.

Perhaps the most significant aspect of the fellows' discussions and their written contributions here is the interdisciplinary applicability of the ideas they explore. Issues investigated in chapters that focus on teaching in the sciences, for example, are vital to instruction in the humanities and social sciences, and vice versa. The chapters of this book reflect the cross-disciplinary "truths" of teaching that the authors considered in their discussions. One crucial theme that weaves itself through the book is the importance of modeling for our students the way we think and question, and then inviting them to engage with us as less experienced colleagues in a shared, scholarly exploration. The first section, **Teaching and Learning in the Classroom**, considers how this collaborative kind of education can be achieved in class meetings in a variety of courses in the humanities, sciences and social sciences. The second section, **Teaching and Learning Beyond the Classroom**, explores ways to continue the collegial dialogue with students outside the confines of the classroom, and to encourage students' ongoing, active determination of their own education.

In addition to these larger unifying themes, more specific concerns connect the chapters in each section. The chapters in **Teaching and Learning in the Classroom** focus on collaborative approaches to problems and ideas. A recurring idea here is the importance of encouraging our students not simply to acquire knowledge, but also to gain the understanding that will help them know when and how to apply their knowledge. In the first chapter, Rebecca Jackman explains how she challenges science students to share her appreciation for the meaning and logic of the formulas they apply to problems. Eric Towne provides another example of how students and a teacher can address a problem jointly, while acknowledging the logic behind their individual strategies. Jackman and Towne share their thought processes with students in chemistry and math courses much as Jennifer Kotilaine does in music courses. Kotilaine describes how this approach helps her to incorporate her own and her students' diverse areas of expertise in the investigation of a musical genre. Leigh Weiss identifies further techniques that encourage a group's exploration of ideas and problems, particularly in the social sciences. There are times when even a teacher's most reliable techniques fail to engage students. Jeffrey Marinacci and James Dawes take on this problem as it affects discussion seminars. My own chapter explores several commonly overlooked considerations that are essential to productive group discussions.

An important theme of the section entitled **Teaching and Learning Beyond the Classroom** is the motivational and educational power of effective feedback for students, particularly on written assignments. This section also addresses particular threats to the collegial, scholarly dialogue between teachers and students, including time constraints, grades and even physical environment. Sujay Rao examines how teachers can best provide feedback on weekly writing assignments, while Kerry Walk explains how students can critique each other's writing constructively. Judith Richardson reflects on how teachers can negotiate the difficult connections between grades, meaningful feedback, criticism and encouragement. Todd Bodner considers these issues in the context of problem-based assignments in quantitative courses. Anne Fernald moves beyond the realm of written comments to consider how, when and where the advice we provide in student-teacher conferences can enhance our students' progress.

The essays compiled here reflect observations the fellows refined jointly in their discussions. These were informed by the participants' own pedagogical experiences and by the publications of the authors on our bibliography. Each chapter benefited initially from the collective experience and critical analysis of the entire group, which includes the authors themselves and also Aimée Bessire, Nina Cannizzaro-Byrne, Lucinda Damon-Bach, Erika Dreifus, Robert Kaplan, David Kidger, Stanley Kurtz, Camille Lizarribar, Ann Reidy, Jerome Reiter, and Elaine Zanutto. In subsequent conversations with the authors, and in successive drafts, I witnessed the ensuing evolutions of their reflections.

The work of many heads, hands and hearts made the Senior Teaching Fellows Program a successful, still ongoing venture and made this publication possible. I am grateful to the entire staff of the Derek Bok Center for Teaching and Learning for their unceasing encouragement and hard work, and particularly to those who commented on early drafts of chapters: Terry Aladjem, Noel Bisson, Alan Cooper, Wendy Franz, John Girash, Virginia Maurer, Jennie Myers, Richard Olivo, Jane Phipps, Allison Pingree, Ellen Sarkisian, and Lee Warren. Most especially, my gratitude goes to every one of the 1996–1997 Senior Teaching Fellows for their commitment and their cooperation in this project.

Mary-Ann Winkelmes
Cambridge, May 1999

TEACHING AND LEARNING
IN THE CLASSROOM

MASTERY VS. MEMORY:
CONCEPTUAL THINKING IN
QUANTITATIVE SCIENCE CLASSES

REBECCA J. JACKMAN

A s an undergraduate, I recall attending an event with many non-scientists, one of whom asked me what my major was. I answered that I was studying chemistry, and her response was, "Oh, that must be hard, so many formulas and equations..." I have realized, during my career as a student and a teacher, that this comment was not far from the truth. I have taken many science classes and have been a teaching assistant (TA) for several others; most classes focused on algorithmic problem solving. The importance of understanding concepts was de-emphasized to the extent that one could pass the exams having only memorized the equations.

Research has suggested that there is a need to modify this current model for teaching in the physical sciences. Several groups have studied both science and non-science majors in first-year chemistry classes to compare their ability to solve a conceptual problem and to solve one that involves the use of algorithms.[1] They find that different students have different ways of learning. Students at the top of the class typically have a grasp of problems both conceptually and algorithmically. There is, however, a large group of reasonably successful chemistry students who are sound algorithmic problem solvers, but who have large gaps in their conceptual understanding. These are the students who could benefit from instruction in conceptual thinking. Similarly, there is a group of students who do best when provided with conceptual problems, but are not as good with equations. These students could potentially be good scientists, but the current model for scientific instruction discourages them from taking other science courses. Striking a balance between problem solving and conceptual thinking could then ideally both engage a broader range of students in science and develop in these students the skills necessary to reason scientifically.

The misplaced emphasis on teaching equations rather than concepts in medium- to large-sized quantitative science classes stems largely, I believe, from the time constraints placed on instructors. First, teaching both concepts and equations takes more time in preparation and class hours, especially if there is dialogue during class. Second, grading three hundred or so exams presents a daunting task even when the questions require right-or-wrong numerical answers. If the exams were to test concepts and demand short written answers, grading would seem an insurmountable task.

Adding to these limitations is the fact that students themselves are often so focused on their short term goal—be it passing the course, finishing the semester or getting a good grade to get into graduate or medical school—they lose sight of the purpose of their undergraduate education. They are not as concerned with learning or gaining a basic understanding of a particular field as with passing the course. By teaching in the present mode, we encourage this practice. They are doing themselves a disservice, and we are facilitating it. Our goal should not be merely to teach the students how to pass or to get through a class, but rather to develop scientific reasoning based on knowledge and understanding of scientific concepts. As educators, we need to realign both our own goals and the goals of our students; we should pose problems so that a student is forced to ask herself, "what is happening physically and how do I solve this problem based on my physical understanding?" rather than, "into which equation should I plug these numbers?"

Given that in any course there is finite quantity of material that must be taught and that we have only a few contact hours per week, how do we, as lecturers or TAs, teach our students to think conceptually? Here I will describe some of my ideas for encouraging conceptual learning within these constraints. Specific examples are drawn from my own experiences teaching chemistry, but it is my hope that they will illustrate ideas that may be valuable to anyone teaching in the physical sciences.

Discouraging the "Plug-and-Chug" Approach

The traditional model for teaching large science classes creates a "plug-and-chug" mentality amongst the students. When faced with an algorithmic problem set, they work to find the right equation, plug the numbers in, and chug through the calculation without *thinking*. Equations in science are derived either empirically or from first principles; as such, they are just a way of summarizing physical reality. Each equation has its basis in a physical phenomenon, some more obvious to the students than others. In the current approach to teaching quantitative science, the equations often become divorced from the physical phenomena that they describe, making it possible for a student to pass a course by memorizing an appropriate set of formulas without really grasping the underlying concepts. Six months after the end of the course, the details of equations fade from memory, particularly if they were crammed the night before the exam. By contrast, conceptual understanding of a phenomenon and the ability to reason scientifically should be less easily lost.

Students using the "plug-and-chug" approach to problem solving often abandon their own common sense. For example, on a problem set in a general chemistry course for which I was a TA, students had to calculate the energy of yellow light and compare it to the energy needed to depress a typewriter key. There was a typographical error in the problem: the value provided for the energy needed to depress a typewriter key was far too small. From the calculation, yellow light—in fact any wavelength of visible light— would cause the typewriter key to be depressed! Of my forty students, however, only *one* person remarked that this answer did not seem to make sense. In this class, the students were assigned conceptual problems each week but when asked specifically to compare two numbers, they were not thinking.

In the same class on an exam, the students were asked to calculate the equilibrium constant for a reaction using the change in Gibbs free energy for that reaction. The equilibrium constant (K) for a reaction tells whether reactants or products are favored; it is mathematically related to the change in Gibbs free energy (DG) that is a measure of the spontaneity of a reaction: if the reaction is spontaneous (DG is negative), the products are favored (K>1), and the reverse is true if DG is positive. In grading the exam, I saw many cases where students had been in "plug-and chug" mode, but in the panic of the exam had omitted a negative sign in the equation relating the two quantities. For a spontaneous reaction, they determined an equilibrium constant that favored reactants. If they had thought for a moment they might have realized their mistake and traced it back to the equation; instead, they moved on to the next problem.

By allowing our students to provide only numerical answers and by accepting these numbers as proof of understanding of concepts, we are not requiring them to think. They can write problem sets and exams on auto-pilot. As a scientist, however, one is constantly asking oneself if the answer to a calculation makes sense. The question is, how do we start to develop this internal querying in our students, the future scientists?

Solving problems during a small class, office hours, or in section (a weekly, small-group class meeting designed to complement lectures) is an ideal time to get students thinking. Once the necessary equation has been identified, I will ask a student to predict roughly what the answer is going to be—for example, is the equilibrium constant going to be greater than or less than one? The ability to estimate numbers or to do quick "back-of-the-envelope" calculations are useful skills to acquire early in a scientific career. Once we have made the calculation, I will pose the question: "Does this answer make sense?"

By requiring that students write a one line justification of each numerical answer that they provide on a problem set, it is possible to continue to instill in the students the need to question, always. Once trained, the students should start to ask themselves these same questions without prompting.

Drawing Parallels and Making Connections

Another trend I have observed in introductory classes is the overwhelming quantity of material that is presented very quickly—I have been a TA for classes where we tried to cover the entire field of thermodynamics in a week! The students are often unsure of where to begin studying. As instructors, with prior knowledge of the material, we should be able to help the students focus their learning by pointing out connections in seemingly disparate material.

The students' problem of not seeing parallels comes partly from text-books that compartmentalize information into discrete chapters. Students tend then to separate the topics in their minds into these same sections. They fail to make connections between related, or sometimes identical, concepts in different guises because they are not looking beyond the equations. Students will say, "there's so much to know for the test: all the gas-phase equilibrium, the acid-base stuff, the solubility chapter...I don't know where to start..." They have not realized that all the topics are manifestations of a *single* phenomenon, equilibrium. By thoughtful presentation of material during our few contact hours, we can start to draw parallels between similar concepts and topics for them and encourage them to make similar connections for themselves.

Relating Back to Physical Phenomena

"I'm having a hard time remembering, when you add sugar to water, do you get boiling point depression or elevation? What was the equation again?" I have had many questions of this sort from students and my response is always: *"you don't have to remember,* you just have to think about what's happening on a molecular level." The gap in conceptual understanding makes learning difficult—students have seen an equation, but do not understand it because they have no sense for the phenomenon that it describes. The approach that I have used to teach students to understand the phenomenon is to work through the concepts in a small class, in section, or during office hours with the students thinking aloud. For example, I will sketch a beaker of water on the board, and ask what the definition of the boiling point is. Eventually, someone will tell me that it is the point at which the vapor pressure equals atmospheric pressure. What determines the vapor pressure, and then what happens to it if I add sugar to the water, I will ask. The dialogue continues in this vein, until we reach the collective conclusion that adding sugar decreases the fraction of water at the interface. This effect lowers the vapor pressure, and so more heat is needed for the vapor pressure to reach one atmosphere. By the end of the conversation, the answer that the boiling point is elevated is obvious to the students. By referencing the equations back to the physical phenomena that they describe, they become less abstract and more comprehensible for the students.

Demonstrating Concepts

Despite the best verbal explanations, some concepts can remain quite abstract and difficult to grasp. Sometimes a simple demonstration can serve to introduce or augment the explanation of a concept. Good demonstrations have the advantage that they have a greater visual impact on the students and may be retained longer than equations presented on a blackboard. The most effective demonstrations are often those where the students participate in the experiment themselves. Once, I was explaining the concept of surface tension, interfacial free energy (a measure of how much two things like to be in contact with one another), and contact angle (a measure of how much a drop of liquid spreads on a surface—related to the interfacial free energies). We discussed the concept and talked about the relevant equations, but there was still something a little too abstract for the students to grasp. Then I passed around a water bottle and a surface that had been treated so that it was like teflon on one half and like glass on the other. The students took turns putting water on the surface and observing that on one side (the teflon-like side) the drops of water beaded up, and on the other they spread to cover the entire surface. The action of "doing" is often key to solidifying our understanding.

Continuing to Refine Understanding of Concepts

Most introductory chemistry courses spend some time studying rates of reaction, or kinetics. One of the concepts that is introduced is the rate determining step (RDS), that is, the slow step in a reaction that determines how fast the overall rate of reaction goes. Ask any upper-level chemistry major, what the RDS of a reaction is and she will say: "the slowest step in the reaction" as she was taught in first-year chemistry. Draw on the blackboard a sketch of the energy profile for a reaction ($A \leftrightarrow B \leftrightarrow C$) where B is less stable than A, and the relative height of the barrier between A and B is larger than that between B and C, but the absolute height of the barrier between B and C is greater (see diagram).

Pose the same question, "what's the RDS for the forward reaction?" as I did last semester, and it will be a different story: the majority of the students will argue, incorrectly, that the first step is slower. Here is a situation where the students believe that they understand a concept but have not thought seriously about what it means. In fact, the intuition that they have developed is wrong. They look at the diagram and their intuition says the step with the largest barrier must be the slow one.

How can we help them to think correctly about a such problem? The way I tried to refine their thinking was to ask them to reconsider what the rate of a reaction really is: it is a measure of the number of molecules that

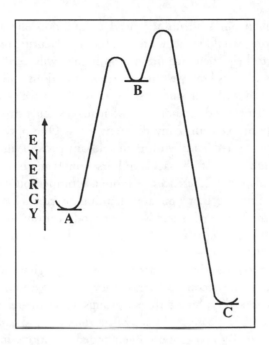

make it over the reaction barrier per unit time. The rate then is determined by two factors: the height of the barrier, as they correctly observed, but also the number of molecules waiting to react. Even if the height of the barrier is low, if there are no molecules present, the reaction rate will be zero! In the case of B going to C, the barrier is low, but the number of B molecules is small because it is a higher energy level. Explained in this way, the concept becomes clear to most of them for the first time. We need to realize, particularly when teaching upper-level classes, that there are often gaps in students' conceptual knowledge where there should not be. Often the TAs for a class are better positioned than the lecturer to notice these deficiencies, but together the lecturer and the TAs can help to remedy them by working to refine the understanding of concepts.

Encouraging Students to Think as Research Scientists

We can instill in our students the need to question all calculations they make, just as they would if they were conducting scientific research. We can do still more to help them acquire the skills they will need as scientists by demonstrating in class how we ourselves pose questions and by sharing our thought processes with our students. To illustrate, if we were interested in testing the students' understanding of what makes acids strong or weak, we could pose the problem in many different ways. One option would be to provide a list of related acids, with their relevant pK_as (a number related to the relative stabilities of the acid and its conjugate base), and ask the students to explain the differences. A more useful method might be to pose the question: imagine that you are planning to run a reaction, but the reaction goes too slowly with acid X. What modifications to the structure of the acid would you suggest to make it more acidic (and therefore make the reaction faster)? Explain why the changes you suggest would make it more acidic. In the first case, the students need only regurgitate what they know about acidity; in the second scenario, they need to recall for themselves what determines acidity, how different groups affect the relative energies of the acid and conjugate base, and what effect they want to cause to make the reaction go faster. By asking more open-ended questions in the same way that they would arise in our own research, we model for the students the skills appropriate for doing science.

As lecturers and teaching assistants, we have the opportunity to make a large impact on the students' learning and training. We can generate both interest in and comprehension of science by conveying our own enthusiasm, knowledge, and manner of thinking/questioning. These ideas for encouraging conceptual learning and understanding will, I hope, be of practical use to both beginning lecturers and teaching assistants wishing to make such an impact by striking a balance between rote problem solving and conceptual teaching.

Selected Bibliography

Nakhleh, Mary B. "Are Our Students Conceptual Thinkers or Algorithmic Problem Solvers?" *Journal of Chemical Education* 70 (January 1993): 50–55.

Nakhleh, Mary B., Lowrey, Kirsten A., & Mitchell, Richard C. "Narrowing the Gap between Concepts and Algorithms in Freshman Chemistry." *Journal of Chemical Education* 73 (August 1996): 758–762.

Nakhleh, Mary B., and Mitchell, Richard C. "Concept Learning versus Problem Solving." *Journal of Chemical Education* 70 (March 1993): 190–192.

Nurrenberg, Susan C. & Pickering, Miles. "Concept Learning versus Problem Solving: Is there a difference?" *Journal of Chemical Education* 64 (June 1987): 508–510.

Phelps, Amy J. "Teaching to Enhance Problem Solving." *Journal of Chemical Education* 73 (April 1996): 301–304.

Pickering, Miles. "Further Studies on Concept Learning versus Problem Solving," *Journal of Chemical Education* 67 (March 1990): 254–255.

Sawrey, Barbara A. "Concept Learning versus Problem Solving: Revised." *Journal of Chemical Education* 67 (March 1990): 253–254.

Tobias, Sheila. *They're not Dumb, They're Different.* Tucson: Research Corporation, 1990.

LECTURES WITHOUT LECTURING: AN INTERACTIVE DISCOVERY OF KEY IDEAS IN MATH AND SCIENCE

ERIC TOWNE

Intuition and creativity were vital in developing many of the key ideas that are taught today in introductory college math and science lecture courses. With a little guidance from the teacher, the students in such courses should be able to use their own intuition and creativity to discover these ideas for themselves, as mathematicians and scientists did originally. Most steps in the development of these concepts are entirely natural and within the reach of college students. However, teaching in a lecture-style format does not encourage students to develop concepts; instead, it lulls them into sitting unthinking, copying down notes without exploring ideas for themselves.

On the other hand, if students are encouraged (and even required) to suggest, criticize, and refine their own ideas during class, the benefits can be immense. The students feel a stronger sense of ownership in the concepts of the course and have a more intimate knowledge of where these concepts came from; this makes it easier for them to re-derive the results for themselves if the need arises later. This method of learning also helps to teach simultaneously the skills of independent thinking and collaborative problem-solving. Finally, if the students derive the results of the course largely on their own, it helps remove some of the mystery that is often attached to a cold, hard formula.

This essay has two main goals. The first is simply to convince the reader that it is possible to teach math and science courses this way by giving a sample of discussion from such a class. The second is to provide a basic framework for giving a lecture without dictating and to offer a few suggestions on what to do and what not to do. The essay will focus on a mathematics class, but the concepts could be applied to virtually any introductory science or mathematics course and perhaps some advanced ones.

The dialogues that are transcribed here occurred in a calculus class at Harvard. As the discussion progressed, the key points were written out on the chalkboard to make it easier for students to enter them in their notebooks. Calculus is not taught in large lectures here, but rather in many separate classes of about 25 students each. The semester was well underway, so the students had grown somewhat accustomed to contributing their own suggestions and ideas in this class. Beginning with the first class meeting, I had told them that they would need to come up with suggestions on how to approach the problems I presented. By asking a wide variety of questions, from quite elementary through very difficult (and including some "trick" questions that I knew virtually everyone would answer incorrectly), I was soon fortunate to have a classroom in which most students felt free to make suggestions and ask questions with little stigma attached to being wrong. In addition, since in most calculus classes there are some students who have already encountered portions of the material, we had many suggestions right from the start. The topic of the day was finding Taylor (polynomial) approximations to functions.

Getting Started

Many educators stress the importance of a good initial question to foster discussion. Luckily, the fields of math and science are full of such questions. It was this very type of question that first motivated people to develop the basic tools we now use in math and science. Most of the major questions in a course, ranging from how to find the velocity of an object to how to model the interaction between two populations to how to describe the motion of a pendulum, provide excellent starting points that arise naturally.

Teacher: If I asked you to compute $e^{1/10}$, how would you do it?
Student 1: With a calculator.
Student 2 (simultaneously): Use a table.
Student 3 (almost simultaneously): From the graph.

This starting question has several good answers that are easy for the students to identify. We are fortunate to have several interesting suggestions so quickly; the small class size and informal atmosphere make the students more willing to speak up. These student contributions also point out the danger in anticipating their responses. In previous semesters, someone had always suggested the use of a slide rule, and I was expecting to start a discussion from this idea; since no one offered this suggestion, I took a different approach.

Now we need to sort out these ideas, preferably by letting the students decide for themselves the merits of each suggestion.

Guiding Without Dictating

Two objectives here can sometimes come into conflict with one another. One goal is to encourage the students to discover for themselves the key concepts of the day's topic; however, another goal is to try to ensure that the class covers the intended material within the hour. To accomplish both, the teacher needs to allow the discussion to flow as freely as possible while using his or her knowledge of the subject to prevent the class from spending too much time on a path that doesn't lead to a useful result.

T: OK, good. Let's look at these options. First, suppose you use a graph. Are there any problems with this?

S4: What if you don't have a graphing calculator? Then what?

T: Right. It would be very hard to draw an accurate graph of the exponential function by hand. How about the idea of using a calculator? Does this raise any new questions?

S5: What if you need more decimal places?

T: Yes. That's one. It would be nice to be able to get as accurate an answer as we want, and that's something we'll look at more closely later. Anything else?

Student 5's response probably isn't going to take us in the direction I hope to go, but it is an important issue that we will need to address again in a few days. For now, she knows that she made a good suggestion, and I will refer to it as her idea when we return to it later.

S6: What if you don't have a calculator?

S2: Then you use a table.

T: What if you don't have a table or a calculator?

S7: Then you're screwed. (Laughter.)

T: Are you? Do you think these computations are impossible without a calculator or a table?

S4: Well, no. I mean, some person had to make the tables in the first place, right?

T: Yes! Exactly! And someone had to program your calculator to spit out the right answers.

S8: We should just ask him how to do it. (More laughter.)

T: That wouldn't be much fun. I think we can figure it out for ourselves.

After only a short detour, we've arrived at one of the key places along the way to the final goal. By answering a few appropriately chosen questions, the students have critiqued and developed their own original thoughts on the subject.

Going Astray/Going Nowhere

Alas, not everything is as smooth as our path above. Sometimes, rephrasing a question makes it easier for the students to see the heart of the problem.

T: What is it about quantities like $e^{1/10}$ or sin 2 or the square root of 11 that makes them so hard for us to calculate?

S1: They're not integers.

T: Yes, but neither are 2/8 or 2/9, and they're easy to calculate.

S4: What do you mean by 'hard'?

T: Well, that's exactly what I'm trying to get you guys to tell me!

I'll spare you the next several suggestions from the class. It is clear that this particular statement of the question is not taking us in the right direction, so I try to reword the question.

T: Let's look at this from a different angle. What kinds of quantities are easy for us to compute?

S1: Things like 2 plus 3.

S9: Or 2 times 3.

T: What is it about these that makes them easy? Is it because the numbers are simple or because the operations are?

S9: Both, really.

T: Well, what about 81 plus 95? Or 81 times 95? Are these harder or just longer to do?

S10: Just longer. It's the same idea as before.

T: Right, it's still addition and multiplication. And what other operations are as easy as these two?

S1: Division and subtraction.

T: Anything else?

S11: Exponents?

T: Really? So, something like $2^{1/2}$ is easy for you to do?

S11: No, I guess not.

T: Yeah, not really. It's the four operations of addition, subtraction, multiplication, and division that are the easiest. And what kinds of functions use just these operations?

S9: Linear functions.

T: True. Can we be broader than that?

S4: Polynomials.

T: Beautiful. Polynomials are very easy to evaluate and they're especially easy for a machine like a computer or a calculator, machines that were built to do lots and lots of additions and multiplications very quickly and very accurately. Polynomials are easy, whereas exponentials and logs and trig functions and square roots are hard. So, if we can't compute the exact value of some hard function, what kind of function could we use to approximate this value?

S4: A polynomial.

T: You got it.

Although some members of the class have certainly followed everything so far, others haven't. Stopping to ask for questions gives the braver students a chance to ask the questions that many of their peers probably share. Ideally, these questions could then be answered by someone other than the teacher, although I don't ask for students to do so here.

T: Does everyone see why a polynomial is easier?

S11: Why do polynomials only use those operations?

T: Well, if we write out any polynomial like this one (writes one on board) then to find out its value at any x, the only thing we need to do is add, subtract, multiply, or divide. Does that make sense?
S11: Yeah.

In not much time and with only limited help from me, the class has come up with the notion of using polynomials to approximate other functions, a key idea in mathematics and one that is used widely in many other fields. Now we need to determine a procedure for choosing the right polynomial to make a given approximation. Things are going a little slowly, so I'll give a small hint with the first question.

T: And how can we decide which polynomial to use? Suppose that we want to estimate $e^{1/10}$ or e raised to some other number near zero. Think about it graphically.
S4: We want a polynomial that looks like e^x.
T: Great. Now let's figure out what 'looks like' should mean. Let's say we're going to use a linear polynomial. What can we control about a linear function?
S1: The slope.
T: Good. What else?
S10: The y-intercept.
T: Exactly. We can choose the slope and the y-intercept to be anything we want. But if we want our linear function to look like e^x near zero, then what should the y-intercept be?
S4: One.
T: Good. Why?
S4: Because that's the y-intercept of e^x.
T: Perfect! And what should the slope of our approximating function be?
S12: The same as the slope of e^x at zero.
T: Exactly. And that slope is one. This is just the idea that we wanted. By matching up the y-intercept and the slope at zero, we can make our function look a lot like e^x near zero.

One student has a good question that I can use to lead into the next topic of discussion.

S2: Wait a second. e^x is curved, right? So why are we using a straight line?

T: You're right. Look at the graph. (Draws it on the board.) Do you see that near zero the graphs are pretty close? But then what happens? They get farther and farther away, so how could we improve on our approximating function?

S2: Make its slope get bigger and bigger.

T: Well, can we make the slope of a linear function different in different places?

S2: No, I guess not.

T: So what can we do instead?

S6: Use another exponential function?

T: Ah, well, remember that it's the exponential functions that are hard to compute and that we're using polynomials to approximate them.

These wrong answers are often great for reminding the class of what our goal is. Looking back, it would have been even better if I had asked someone in the class to explain why we wouldn't want to use another exponential function.

S4: So use a parabola or something.

T: Exactly. Because now a parabola lets us match up the y-intercept, the slope, and what else?

S4: The concavity.

T: Right. In fact, we can use a polynomial of any degree we like. The higher the degree, the more things beyond concavity we can make match up with the other function we're trying to approximate and the better an approximation we can get.

Hooray! The class has arrived at the big idea of the day, a method of how to choose polynomials to approximate other functions. I hope that they feel some ownership in the ideas since they have done this largely by themselves and with just a little guidance from me. I also hope that by discussing a variety of ideas (especially the ones that didn't work) instead of just watching me put 'the right ideas' on the board, the students have a clearer sense of why this process of approximation works and why we selected the ideas we ended up using. Using this type of non-lecture format throughout the semester, I hope to help the students learn something about thinking creatively in math and the sciences and also something about how mathematicians and scientists brainstorm and develop ideas.

Moving On: From the Abstract to the Concrete

Now we need to reinforce what we've learned by going through some specific examples of polynomial approximations rather than the abstract generalities we've been discussing so far. During these specific examples, the students will do an even greater portion of the talking than they have already because the hard part (when creativity and intuition were necessary) is over. The students who had been making most of the suggestions so far will need less guidance from me and will be able to see more of the steps for themselves as they take the abstract ideas they've already developed and apply them to some concrete functions; for the others, the concrete examples provide both an opportunity to clarify ideas of which they are still unsure and a second chance to ask questions.

Getting Everyone Involved

In courses I have taught this way, typically about fifty percent of the students in the class participate on any given day. Unfortunately, it tends to be nearly the same fifty percent in every class meeting. Nevertheless, this means that many more people are contributing to the class than would be if the students were simply being dictated to. To get non-speaking students a little more involved, one can always call on people who have not volunteer-ed. Alternatively, I have often asked for several predictions about what answer we should expect before completing a problem and then had the entire class vote on which prediction they thought most accurate.

Possible Drawbacks

There are, of course, some dangers to teaching math or science in this way. Probably the most common is that the discussion proceeds so slowly or ranges so far afield that it is clear that the pace will not exhaust the topic in the allotted time. At worst, this means that the teacher has to tighten the discussion and resort to something more like classic lecturing in order to cover the material. But it is usually possible to adopt a less extreme solution of merely giving more explicit guidance and filtering the students' suggestions to select those that are most on track. Another danger comes from the fact that most students are not accustomed to learning math in this manner. As a result, some will feel frustrated initially at what they perceive to be a lack of structure in the presentation. However, after a few successful classes, they usually see that we do actually get the math done and they become more accepting of the non-lecturing approach; furthermore, I try to summarize the day's key ideas in a few minutes at the end of each class. And the unease felt by these students is usually outweighed by the enthusiasm felt by most of the others. I am still inspired by a student who said midway through the first class I taught, "It's so cool to be learning math this way!"

"NOT IN MY VILLAGE": REFLECTIONS ON BRINGING MUSICAL CULTURE TO THE DIVERSE CLASSROOM

JENNIFER B. KOTILAINE

After two weeks of preparation—through reading, watching video tapes, and practicing while pacing in time around my apartment: clapping, stomping, clicking my tongue, and driving my husband crazy—I finally thought I had learned enough about the Ghanaian drumming tradition to teach Drum Gahu patterns to my students in an African music course.[1] Designed for non specialists, the course was nevertheless a challenging one for me to teach, as I had very little prior experience with African music. So far, my extensive (Western) musical training had sufficed, and I thought I was managing to "wing it" quite well. Standing in front of my seventeen students, I showed them the rhythmic pattern associated with the particular instruments: the gankogui, the axtase, the sogo, the kidi, and the kaganu. I had the students drum out each of the separate patterns on their desks, and then eventually divided them up into smaller groups, each of which was assigned a particular part. We thus performed our own rendition of Drum Gahu, switching parts every few minutes so that each group could have a chance to "play" each part. The students welcomed the change from the usual lecture mode and I, too, felt the excitement of getting the students to participate actively in a tradition. The hour was almost over and I tried to bring the class back to a concluding discussion, hoping to make the point that perhaps we had gained a better understanding of what constitutes Ghanaian drumming. Sitting, as per usual, in a back corner of the room, an especially quiet student raised his hand. "How thrilling," I thought, "this exercise has been so successful, now even *he* wants to participate!" Relishing the tiny personal breakthrough, I almost didn't hear what the student was actually saying. "I come from Ghana, and this isn't how we drum at all. Not in my village."

None of my graduate courses in ethnomusicological history, theory, and method had prepared me for this moment, this obvious public challenge to my authority. After all, with what authority was I teaching this course, anyway? I was neither a scholar of African music, nor a performer, nor even a consumer of it and—even worse—compounding my inexperience was a perception on the part of many of my students that I, as a white graduate student, couldn't possibly have anything to offer them. With every good intention, some students told me explicitly in private meetings that I couldn't possibly teach this course "correctly" because I was neither from Africa nor of African descent and thus would be somehow "genetically incapable" of understanding the material.[2] When I would raise the example of an African-American teaching assistant for the course who was writing her dissertation on neither an African nor an ethnomusicological topic, but rather on Verdi operas, students assured me that she nevertheless had a kind of "innate connection" to the material that I could never acquire. "Please don't be offended," students of all races would always say, "it's just that, no matter how hard you try, you'll never quite get it."

Although I had been reading as much as possible on African music, history, and aesthetics, and in spite of my frantic preparations before each section (a weekly, small-group class meeting designed to complement lectures), I still had not won the full confidence of the students. Certainly, they respected my observations, since I already had over two decades' worth of training in refining the way I both listen to and understand music. I was able to employ specific technical vocabulary that can be used to describe any kind of musical tradition (such as the nature of meter, rhythm, dynamics, texture, speed, range, etc.) and students recognized that I could at least teach them to process intelligently what they heard, rather than letting the sound just wash over them. Furthermore, I had established my credibility as a musicologist aware of her Western musical biases at the beginning of the term in a way I had not expected. Directly after the first musical excerpt I played in the first day of class, a student shouted out to ask, "Why is this music so goddamn out of tune?" The room fell absolutely still. I took a deep breath and explained that part of our work in this course was in learning to evaluate the music that we hear in as universal a way as possible and that in order to do this, we were going to have to get away from hearing musical sound only through Western ears and expectations. I then went on to explain that there are many systems of tuning musical instruments, and that our organization of pitches into scales made up of tones and semitones was a product of Western tradition, and ultimately just as arbitrary as any other.

Despite my very best efforts, I almost reached a breaking point with Drum Gahu. In the expectant silence that followed the student's refutation of my presentation, I was faced with a very distinct choice: either let my insecurities—fueled by student doubt—get the better of me, or do my best to confound all of our (low) expectations in order to do justice not only to the material, but also to the students and even myself. While the teacher in me was annoyed (hurt, frustrated) by the situation in which I found myself, I chose instead to respond as an ethnomusicologist, rejoicing that I had found another "informant" to aid me/us in my/our work. In other words, I took the "not in my village" remark not as a slight, but rather as an opportunity. Asking the student if he might share his experiences of making music in his village in Ghana, I relinquished control, allowing the student to be the teacher momentarily. As he began to describe the music-making in his village, I watched as the students looked at their classmate with new interest and respect. I encouraged them not to waste their chance to be ethnomusicologists, allowing them to ask questions directly of their colleague, while I posed some of my own.

As the discussion continued, I realized that in spite of my commitment and preparation, I was wrong to think that I was the only one who had anything to offer. All the books, videos, and tapes in the world could not possibly replace the treasures I had sitting in front of me in the classroom. I began to scan the syllabus along with my attendance book, my mind racing: this student was from Ethiopia...that would be handy next week, another student from Senegal might contribute to the Kora unit...the Nigerian would perhaps have something to say about Jùjú...and it would be interesting to engage the South African students in a discussion of Mbube....The most important thing was to step away from the instructional model I had constructed in my head, where the exchange of the information flowed only from teacher to student. By effectively conducting ethnomusicological research in the classroom, I could not only ensure a two-way flow of information, but I could also demonstrate for the students something of how the discipline of ethnomusicology is practiced.

An additional benefit of this approach was that students gradually became more critical of the readings, now that they could compare notes with the experiences of a "native." In each class meeting, the "informant-of-the-week" would be asked to be the first to respond to the readings, which would then prompt a more general discussion about the many difficult issues ethnomusicologists face in both accurately representing and analyzing a given tradition in the context of scholarship. Redirecting the focus from me as musical expert and instructor to all of us in these discussions as either inquisitive ethnomusicologists or resident experts gradually created a distinct sense of community in our classroom.

The mutual respect and trust that developed between us was most vivid at the end of the semester, when we started discussing Zulu isikhunzi music. I explained the derivation of the word "isikhunzi" from a derogatory racial epithet ("coon"), which was consciously co-opted by early twentieth-century Zulu singers as a badge of pride. Cautiously, I then asked the students if they could think of any other instances in which such a phenomenon might occur. To my relief, students responded to this question without restraint, and were able to discuss their use of words like "niggah," "jewboy," "queer," and "dyke" with a great deal of seriousness and candor, probing each other for further explanations or respectfully disagreeing. Remembering all of our concerns at the beginning of the semester, I smiled as we tackled the unspeakable.

During the course of the semester, the students' commitment and enthusiasm vis-à-vis the material helped create a "village" of our very own, a classroom environment where "researchers" and their "subjects" could interact in a way that maintained the integrity of both parties. Demonstrating the tools (and issues) of the ethnomusicological trade—while dealing with musical repertories and concepts—encouraged informed critical thinking among the students, a skill that would serve them well even outside the confines of ethnomusicology. Finally, my departure from the unidirectional model of teacher-student interaction facilitated a more honest and productive means of information sharing, one where each person in the classroom had responsibility for the progress of the group's education, a private stake in the welfare of our village. As individuals, we had left behind our low expectations; as a village, we were a success.

FOUR TECHNIQUES THAT BRIDGE THE BARRIERS TO KNOWLEDGE SHARING IN THE CLASSROOM

LEIGH M. WEISS

Knowledge has been proposed as a central feature of post-industrial society,[1] and knowledge sharing—the interactive communication of ideas, insights, and experiences—has been associated with enormous benefits to individuals, groups, and organizations. The benefits of knowledge sharing have been chronicled in business settings as well as classroom contexts. These benefits include enhanced individual and group motivation, productivity, creativity, satisfaction, the appreciation of diversity and multiple perspectives, and learning.[2]

Although the benefits of knowledge sharing have been widely extolled, there are often considerable barriers to attaining it. In classroom contexts, one of the main barriers is the allocation of credit for ideas. Incentive systems like individual grades for students and forced grade curves can undermine the goals of knowledge sharing and collaboration. Additionally, teaching approaches that emphasize and reinforce individual performance to the exclusion of collaborative learning also inhibit knowledge sharing among students. How can these common barriers to knowledge sharing among students be overcome? This chapter addresses this question by presenting four techniques that overcome the barriers to knowledge sharing and build bridges to collaborative learning.

The four techniques that will be described here—brainstorming, barn raising, point/counterpoint arguing, and scenario visioning—facilitate knowledge sharing among students. They draw on participant input as the foundation for collaborative learning. In most cases, these techniques are broadly applicable to a wide range of subject areas and can be employed to teach material on a continuum from introductory to advanced.

Brainstorming

Perhaps the most familiar of the four techniques, brainstorming is a group process for generating many ideas. Osborn's (1957) book *Applied Imagination*[3] instigated the spread of brainstorming as a technique for increasing creativity. He proposed four key rules for brainstorming sessions: don't criticize others, encourage quantity in the production of ideas, combine and improve ideas suggested by others, and say all ideas that come to mind, no matter how wild.[4]

Brainstorming can be applied to a wide variety of subject areas, and is particularly useful for problem-solving exercises. For example, students in an introductory course on the sociology of organizations for which I was a teaching fellow (TF) used brainstorming to generate ideas about the reasons for gender inequality in the workplace, and recommendations for addressing this problem. During one discussion, I asked students to volunteer ideas from course lectures, readings, and their own experiences, and recorded each idea on the chalk board. Writing down student ideas so every one could see them lent legitimacy to each idea, communicated the message that there are no "wrong" answers, and enabled students who tended to take more time to think before speaking to see the progression of the discussion and reflect on ideas already contributed before suggesting their own. As soon as a couple of students advanced ideas, others followed with a rush of contributions until the three chalk boards in the room were nearly filled. Some students would build on ideas that had already been suggested, while others would develop new angles.

We began the brainstorming session by generating ideas about why gender inequality occurs. The session started with one student suggesting that differences in the behavior of men and women in organizations are biological, arguing that "men and women are wired differently and have different strengths and weaknesses." Another student suggested that "men tend to promote other men, like themselves, and that this group maintains a vice grip on leadership positions by controlling promotions." A third student said, "That idea makes me think of a related reason for inequality, namely that the role models for men and women develop differently because of differences in the positions they hold." Once we had explored the reasons for gender inequality, we held a related brainstorming session centered on recommendations for addressing this problem.

Brainstorming can also be used to generate ideas about how to solve a math or economics problem, address an ethical or political dilemma, design an effective research strategy, or develop a new computer program. The technique can be used in introductory or advanced courses.

While the primary goal of brainstorming is to generate many ideas, this technique can help achieve additional learning-related objectives. First, if Osborn's four rules of brainstorming are enforced, students can volunteer ideas without fearing evaluation. Consequently, the group as a whole benefits from everyone sharing their ideas. Second, brainstorming teaches students how to build on the ideas of others and supports shared understanding and joint responsibility for an outcome. While this approach contrasts with more individualistic approaches to learning, where students develop ideas independently, it can foster the appreciation of diverse viewpoints and collaborative learning. In my experience, brainstorming is also one of the most effective ways of eliciting the participation of everyone in the class and setting norms about respecting others' ideas.[5]

Barn Raising

Barn raising discussion sessions have their origins in frontier America. When a family needed a barn but had limited labor and resources to build it, the entire community would gather to accomplish the task. The family might describe the kind of barn it wanted, and the community would come together to build it, suggesting changes and improvements as the structure was erected. Barn raising discussion sessions begin with a member of the class venturing ideas that may be newly formed and not fully formulated. The rest of the group then builds on the idea, embellishing it and suggesting changes and improvements, just as in the case of building a real barn. Once an idea has been offered by a group member, he or she has no more responsibility for developing, defending, or explaining it than anyone else in the group.[6] In contrast to brainstorming, where one of the main goals is for participants to generate as many ideas as possible, barn raising asks participants to collectively build something from a single idea or set of ideas.

Like brainstorming, barn raising can be applied to a variety of subjects. For instance, I used this approach in a class discussion on job enrichment in the workplace that followed a case study reading assignment about dissatisfied workers in an insurance company. I began by asking one student to venture an idea about how to overcome this problem. The student suggested that work must be meaningful for employees to feel satisfied. Rather than evaluate the suggestion or generate alternative solutions, others in the class were asked to build on the stated idea. Students explored what might constitute "meaningful work," suggesting the importance of skill variety, employee identification with the task being performed, and belief in the importance of the task. From the initial suggestion about "meaningful work" the class designed a program to address the problem of dissatisfied workers presented in the case study.

Barn raising can be used to "build" solutions to problems in math, chemistry, economics, and even the analysis of literature or poetry. It can also be used in conjunction with brainstorming, where brainstorming is used to generate ideas, and barn raising is used to develop one or a number of solutions. Barn raising draws on student input, encourages collaborative work, and emphasizes creativity. One important advantage of this technique is that students do not come away from barn raising sessions holding on to their original ideas. This technique contrasts with more traditional approaches to teaching where students take a position and are asked to defend it. The effect of such a debate or "boxing match" is often the entrenchment of original ideas, rather than the freeing or unfreezing of attitudes and thoughts.[7]

Point/Counterpoint Arguing

This technique modifies the debate or "boxing match" approach to overcome the problem of idea entrenchment, facilitate knowledge sharing, and encourage students to be open to multiple perspectives on an issue. The first step of point/counterpoint arguing involves individual students or groups of students developing a position about an argument, problem, or situation. Other students or groups of students develop different (or counter) positions. Students may be given time during a class to develop a position, or can be asked to do so as a homework assignment between classes. Each position is then presented. The second step involves asking all or some of the individuals or groups to switch positions and argue the position of another individual or group. Again, students may be given time in class or as a homework assignment to prepare the opposite position. If students are told that they will be evaluated on both of the arguments they advance, they will be unlikely to sabotage their initial argument by weakening it.

I have used this technique with students who debated the strengths and weaknesses of teams with supervisors and autonomous teams that operate without supervisors. One group of students was asked to argue the position that groups function more effectively when they have supervisors; the other group of students was asked to argue the opposite. In the initial preparation of the arguments, each group suggested a set of reasons why one team-based approach was better than the other. When the groups were asked to switch positions, they generated responses to issues that only came to light once the first arguments had been advanced. For instance, the group arguing for the merits of autonomous teams without supervisors suggested that the teams would benefit from having control over their own decisions. After the arguments were presented and the groups switched positions, the group arguing for supervised teams suggested that autonomous teams might informally allocate authority to a leader anyway, and that the informal process might engender more resentment than if the supervisor had been clearly appointed in the first place.

Like the other techniques, point/counterpoint arguing can be applied broadly to diverse subject areas and can be used in introductory or advanced courses. I have seen this technique used successfully in law school classes, where students develop a position on a court case, and in philosophy classes, where students argue a particular point of view, and then switch sides. Point/counterpoint arguing draws on student input and can involve collaborative learning, especially if positions or arguments are developed in groups. This technique encourages knowledge sharing by asking students to exchange and respond to each other's arguments. While the main goal of this exercise is to encourage students to learn from each other, a related advantage is that students can see the strengths of different points of view. When students are asked to switch sides of a debate, or argue a different position, they are helped to see the weaknesses in their original position because they must point out the demerits of the original position to develop a strong alternative argument.

Scenario Visioning

This technique is a disciplined method for imagining possible futures and is particularly useful for problem-solving exercises in situations where there is no "right" answer. It involves the identification of basic trends and uncertainties, and the construction of a series of scenarios or stories to justify and explain possible outcomes. While this technique has been used extensively in corporate settings to determine strategies, it can also be used in classroom discussion settings to facilitate knowledge sharing and collaborative learning.

Scenario visioning involves several basic steps. First, the group should identify a focusing question. A good focusing question should be crisp and have sharp, discrete answers. The instructor may wish to suggest a question, and students may be invited to modify it. Second, participants generate ideas (using the brainstorming technique) about important forces and factors that will dictate the answer to the focusing question. These ideas should be written down, and visible to all in the room. Third, the *most important* driving forces (those that will have the most impact on the answer to the focusing question) should be selected from the list generated in the second step. Participants then vote for the most important force. Fourth, the *most uncertain* driving force should be identified from the list generated in the second step. The most uncertain force will be the one whose magnitude, direction, and effect on the driving question is least predictable. Fifth, the most important and most uncertain driving forces are placed on perpendicular axes and made visible to all in the room. Sixth, participants break into four groups to develop scenarios or stories for each of the four quadrants of the axis. Finally, each of the four groups presents its scenario to the others, and the entire group discusses the implications of the different scenarios for the driving question or problem.

Scenario visioning can be applied to many issues or problems. It might be applied in an astronomy class to generate scenarios about how to study planetary developments or changes in the solar system, or a course on the environment to discuss the evolution of the earth's eco-system and consider policy recommendations, or even a film class to discuss possible ways to advertise and promote a new film. Scenario visioning could be used in an economics class, for example, where students consider a case study of a small business trying to decide how much money to borrow under certain circumstances (step 1). After generating ideas about the critical forces that would have an impact on the answer to the driving question (step 2), students might determine the most important force in determining the answer to the question was how much demand there would be for the product (step 3), while the most uncertain force might be inflation rates (step 4). The following two axes would then be juxtaposed (step 5):

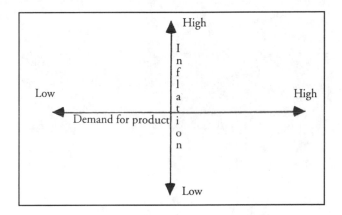

Students would then break into four groups, and each of the groups would develop a scenario based on these forces. The four groups would then present the scenarios to the entire group (step 6), and discuss them (step 7).

Scenario visioning facilitates knowledge sharing and collaborative learning in at least four ways. First, it enables the consideration of a wide variety of issues and perspectives that may be important in solving a particular problem. It thus draws on student inputs and the sharing of diverse perspectives. Second, it avoids tunnel vision, rush to judgment, and adoption of one position, often the one that is most forcefully argued. Third, this approach builds a common language and understanding of issues, without stifling diversity. Fourth, it takes advantage of differences of opinion when multiple perspectives have merit.[8]

These four techniques help overcome some of the main barriers to knowledge sharing by building bridges for collaborative learning. As knowledge gains increasing importance as the main factor of production in our society, working collaboratively and sharing knowledge are becoming essential skills. These abilities are two of the workplace qualities most frequently identified by organizations as essential for future employees because they enable employees to work toward creative solutions to problems.[9] By finding ways to facilitate knowledge sharing and collaborative learning in the classroom we will not only help our students with their studies; we will also help prepare them for life beyond the classroom.

Selected Bibliography

Argyris, Chris and Schö, Donald A. *Organizational Learning II: Theory, Method, and Practice.* Reading, MA: Addison-Wesley, 1996.

Baloche, L. "Breaking Down the Walls: Integrating Creative Questioning and Cooperative Learning into the Social Studies." *Social Studies* 85 (1994): 25–30.

Bell, D. *The Coming of Post-industrial Society: A Venture in Social Forecasting.* New York: Basic Books, 1973.

Hamm, M. *The Collaborative Dimensions of Learning.* Norwood, NJ: Ablex Publishing Corporation, 1992.

Huber, G. "Organizational Learning: The Contributing Processes and the Literatures." *Organization Science* 2 (1991): 88–115.

Levitt, B. and March J. "Organizational Learning." *Annual Review of Sociology* 14 (1988): 319–40.

McCormick, D. and Kahn, M. "Barn Raising: Collaborative Group Process in Seminars." In *Teaching and the Case Method*, 3rd ed., pp. 194–98. Edited by L. B. Barnes; Christensen, C. R.; and Hansen, A. J. Boston: Harvard Business School Press, 1994.

Osborn, A. F. *Applied Imagination.* 2nd ed. New York: Scribner, 1957.

Schoemaker, P. "Scenario Planning: A Tool for Strategic Thinking." *Sloan Management Review* Winter (1995): 25–40.

Sutton, R. I. and Hargadon, A. "Brainstorming Groups in Context: Effectiveness in a Product Design Firm." *Administrative Science Quarterly* 41 (1996): 685–718.

Wack, P. "Scenarios: Shooting the Rapids." *Harvard Business Review* (November-December 1985): 139–150.

Wilson, B. "Dynamic Learning Communities: An Alternative to 'Designed Instructional Systems'." In *Proceedings of Selected Research and Development Presentations at the 1996 National Convention of the Association for Educational Communications and Technology (18th)* Indianapolis, IN: n.p., 1996.

When Good Teaching Techniques Stop Working

JEFFREY MARINACCI

After a summer devoted to research and writing, you realize that classes are starting up next week. You pull out your sheaf of time-tested lesson plans and browse through them in the days before classes begin. Scanning your files, you survey the reading list and your notes. You review the in-class assignments and other teaching and learning devices that you regularly used. You glance through the list of discussion questions that you provided the students prior to each class, and recall that last year's class went well. The students were good; discussions were animated. Everyone learned a lot. Perhaps your teaching had been recognized in previous years. So, with a bundle of notes in hand, you head in to the semester confident that your classes will go well.

After three or four weeks, however, you realize that something is wrong, that the class is not working. Discussions are dull. The students are more concerned with clarifying basic points than thinking through the material in a more sophisticated manner. In-class assignments and other techniques that worked well now bomb.

Regrettably, this describes my own experience teaching a small, introductory social science seminar. Required of sophomore majors, the seminar provides the first in-depth exposure to the discipline. It is the first place where the students can engage in debates and assimilate the analytical and critical skills that mark the discipline. The class is discussion-based, and my lesson plan included teaching techniques that facilitate student participation and a more active approach to learning. Having taught the same course the previous two years, I thought that I had everything in place.

Certainly, external pressures can contribute to this kind of experience. First, no matter what stage of one's career—from graduate student through full professor—there are ubiquitous academic demands: departmental exams, dissertation work, research and publishing, tenure review, committee work, and beyond. In order to meet these demands, we must often make sacrifices. Because it generally ranks low among factors affecting academic progress, teaching may seem a logical sacrifice. Time spent preparing lesson plans and reflecting upon one's purpose as a teacher may be cut to relieve the pressure. Yet by relying upon the time-tested and well-traveled paths of previous efforts, a teacher unilaterally sends the class in a particular direction rather than choosing a path created jointly by teacher and students.

My own vanity, and my reliance on my reputation as a good teacher, initially encouraged me to pursue ineffective remedies for the problem I faced in my social science methodology seminar. My initial decision to wait it out for four weeks was based primarily on two interrelated motivations. I rationalized the problem away by recalling that previous classes had also gotten off to a slow start and by believing that my past success in teaching would see the class through. Naturally, waiting it out didn't change the basic dynamics that impeded effective teaching and learning.

My next approach was to decide that this group of students was not as able as groups from past years. Regardless of discipline, I continually hear teachers comment about students being inadequately prepared or intellectually incapable of mastering a course. This explanation of poor class performance emerges from a self-protective reflex which places all the blame on the students. While such an attitude may be reassuring to faculty, many students have told me that they recognize when their teacher has abandoned them and that thereafter they merely endure the course in frustration or anger.

My third strike at the problem was to find a quick fix by trying new teaching techniques and styles, thereby hoping to reinvigorate the classroom. In this effort, I made the error of emphasizing the "how to" over the "why." That is, I applied these new methods mechanically, without fully considering their appropriateness or rationale. Thus when I added a few tricks for the fourth week of class, my students did not respond positively. Instead, they became even more confused.

After these three failed attempts to address a problem that I had diagnosed as resting with my students, I began to look harder at myself. With trusted colleagues and a valued mentor, I reflected on the fundamental elements of my teaching and academic identity. Why do I think and teach the way that I do? What do I seek to accomplish when I work? How do I ask questions? What kinds of questions are they? What assumptions do I bring to my work? What excites me?

By questioning myself in this manner, I realized that my efforts with my seminar did not reflect who I was as a scholar. As scholars, it is natural to forget the struggle that we endured while learning how to think and organize material as prescribed by our disciplines. Becoming more familiar with the material and adept at the techniques of a discipline is a measure of scholarly progress. But that is not the measure of a teacher's progress. Teachers succeed as they grow more adept at *conveying* a discipline's fundamental skills and principles to students and at helping those students to master them.

I decided to discuss the situation directly with my students. As frightening as that may sound, I am convinced that whatever improvements there were in the classroom emerged from this discussion. I began the discussion by expressing my concerns and clearly stating that the problem was a collective one but that I, as the teacher, had a particular responsibility in its resolution. I then explained what I wished to accomplish in the course. As if it were the first class, I introduced the central principles and debates of the discipline and identified the specific skills that I hoped they would learn in the course. I spoke of my purpose as both a teacher and a scholar and how my teaching ought to reflect the way the discipline works. In essence, I presented them with a clearer picture of my own identity as a teacher and a scholar.

My own frankness encouraged students to speak freely about the situation in turn. For twenty minutes or more, I listened to them vent their frustrations, express their concerns and opinions, and raise questions about many aspects of the class. They told me that they had been struggling with the material from the start. They expressed frustration at not being able to see the connections across the course. They were uncertain how to approach the material. My students had not seen the connections because I had not clearly established the fundamental principles of the discipline nor adequately explained the analytical and critical skills embedded in them. Being able to see connections requires some familiarity with a discipline. But given our poor start, my students had not been able to incorporate these principles and skills into their own academic repertoire.

The success of our join efforts taught me that a frank discussion with students can be the first step in creating a situation in which students begin to struggle with a discipline. Continued discussions of this type help me and my students to keep fundamental principles and skills in view so that the students can wrestle with them as they create their own academic identity.

Selected Bibliography

Hackman, J. Richard, ed. *Groups That Work (and Those That Don't): Creating Conditions for Effective Teamwork.* San Francisco: Jossey-Bass, 1990.

McKeachie, Wilbert. *Teaching Tips: Strategies, Research, and Theory for College and University Teachers.* Lexington, MA: D.C. Heath, 1994.

Parker, Palmer J. "Good Talk about Good Teaching: Improving Teaching through Conversation and Community." *Change* 25 (November-December 1993): 8–13.

Losing It and Getting It Back:
A Teacher's Basics for Leading Seminars

JAMES R. DAWES

An actor loses his voice because he has taken to skipping warm-ups; a highly trained athlete strains a muscle because she has begun to minimize the amount of time she spends on basic calisthenics. Or a writer ceases producing works of excellence because she has come to rely upon her experience rather than upon the painstaking exercises and procedures she had used to motivate herself as a beginner. I hope this may resonate with some of your own experiences.

The more we do something the less rewarding it becomes; often it is less rewarding because the outcomes of our performance are of diminished quality. We lose "it" because we have forgotten the basics, or because we have assumed we can get away without them. This essay is about a teacher's basics. It is, so to speak, the seminar leader's calisthenics, a list of concepts and techniques that we have learned, used, and, in some cases, decided we can do without. There is nothing so dispiriting for teacher or for student as a seminar in which questions fall flat, conversation drifts aimlessly, and a small number of predictable voices predominate. The following strategies are about how to get students to talk; more importantly, they are about how to get them to talk with intelligence and enthusiasm. These techniques are designed to create a classroom environment in which students feel safe to express their ideas freely and to risk being wrong. Very broadly, they can be grouped into four conceptual frameworks: the establishment of bridge-speech structures; the evacuation of power; deroutinization, or the institutionalization of instability; and the ritualization of recognition.[1]

Bridge-speech

The concept of bridge-speech is premised upon the idea that students often need the assistance of supporting language or discursive structures such as an example or preparatory model to move from silence to full participation in the colloquy. Bridge-speech activities can be used at the beginning of the semester to bring students into the conversation and at the end to help them lead it.

Small-group Exercises
Within the first few weeks, you might try designing and implementing an exercise that requires breaking students off into small groups for discussion. This enables the more shy students to try out their voices, so to speak, in a smaller, safer setting; it also helps the students to get to know each other better and consequently can improve the overall dynamic. The discussions ideally should center around specific, preferably written instructions which you will provide, taking them through the steps of analysis necessary for a fruitful discourse. You might, for instance, provide them with a series of questions, or give them a thesis and ask them to put together two or three arguments both in favor of and against it. You might provide broad suggestions for how such arguments might take shape, or point to specific textual moments which are especially relevant. Most importantly, students should be aware that they will be required to report back towards the end of the class and report their findings to the group as a whole.

Collaborative Restatement
In a classroom the conversational ideal is not triangulated: in other words, talk passes freely between the students rather than, after each statement, returning to the gravitational center of the teacher. But a generous restatement of what a student has said ("Let me see if I get what you're saying...") can be very helpful, particularly if the student's comments have been confused, leaving the speaker feeling insecure and the class feeling in the dark. Putting a new spin on their comments, or even reinventing them slightly, while always attributing the ideas to them or their original inspiration, can do much to improve a group dynamic. Such blending of voices and ideas can also help students to see that opinions need not be conceived of as static "property." In other words, you can help to establish through your example a transitional space for students between the extremes

of agreeing in silence and disagreeing through counterpoint, a space for "developing" ideas which belong to the class as a whole.

Student Presentations

In the second half of the semester, when students have become comfortable with the dynamic and class method, you might experiment with allowing your students to run the classroom. For instance, you could parcel out to students the task of opening the class with a brief presentation that is designed to set the framework for subsequent discussion. The principle of bridge-speech is very important here. Some students will do brilliantly under any circumstances; others will not without guidance. The disparity in quality could establish an invidious atmosphere in the classroom. It is important to provide detailed instructions and an explanation of what a presentation ought to look like. Setting a focused, limited range for the presentations can help students feel more in control of the project.

Evacuation of Power

Making an effort to unbuild the hierarchies inherent to the classroom setting (hierarchies of knowledge, voice, and space) can be very useful, so long as one does not go so far as to undermine one's own authority.

Invitational and Inquisitorial Questions

If students feel as if the questions presented to them have single right or wrong answers, they may be very hesitant to speak up. The embarrassment of being wrong outweighs the approbation of being right. Insofar as it is possible, try to ask questions without right or wrong answers, favoring instead those which have a wide latitude for interpretation. "What do you think?" is better than "What is?" "What are some of the relevant qualities of the figure we are discussing?" is better than "Is the figure we are discussing specifically this or that?"

Democratization of Voices

We all, of course, attempt to direct discussion so that no single voice dominates and similarly, so that no single side of the classroom dominates. For this it is important to let your students know from the start that this is your goal—the more transparent your intentions, the more likely you are to receive their cooperation. Attempting to draw out quiet students is always difficult. Most students will rise to the occasion when asked to speak, particularly if the question presented gives them wide latitude, but some will remain steadfastly silent. You might talk to these shy students outside of class, encouraging them to use the seminar as a chance to practice public speaking and asking them what you can do to help them feel more comfortable. You might propose to them, for instance, that they think in advance about a question which you will ask in the next class meeting.

Body and Space
Used in moderation, active, affirmational body language can be instrumental in establishing a comfortable atmosphere. Raising your eyebrows, nodding your head or tilting it to the side, and maintaining eye contact with the speakers are all ways of showing curiosity and interest. Hunching over or resting your chin upon your hands can inhibit your ability to project your voice and enunciate clearly; and negative gestures, like leaning predominately to one side of the classroom or crossing your arms across your chest, can be off-putting to students. Spatial arrangements are likewise of basic importance. The ideal classroom setting is of course the circle; second best is a class that allows you to see the face of each student at all times; least desirable is a room which situates you behind some sort of desk or lectern, effectively insulating you from the students.

Deroutinization

Conversational patterns can quickly ossify. When they do, creative energies can end up being channeled in narrow, rigid, and increasingly familiar ways. It is best not to allow class format to get into a predictable rut, for one's own sake as well as for the students'. Teachers burn out and students get bored when repetition is the rule. If class tends to run so that the whole group discusses one topic together, try breaking them into small groups occasionally. Some weeks let them come into class simply having done the assigned readings; other weeks give them written material a few days in advance, emphasizing what issues and questions they ought to be ready to discuss. The greater the variety the better. Use the blackboard: draw pictures, create diagrams, at the beginning of class write up mysterious phrases or key words which will pique their interest and become clear as the discussion proceeds. If you teach literature, perhaps you could spend some time reading poetry by candlelight; if you teach history, you might schedule one class to run like a courtroom debate, assigning sides to particular groups and giving them time to prepare in class for the discussion which will follow.

The Ritualization of Recognition

It is of course important to memorize students' names as early in the semester as possible. The easiest way to do this is to commit them to memory as they come up—for instance, when a student visits you in office hours, or speaks out in class. Students, however, ought not to feel like they need to *earn* recognition, and they should not have the option of remaining quietly anonymous. Usually more productive, then, is the painstaking and initially cumbersome process of memorizing the names of all students in your class collectively on the first day. As a supplement, it can be very useful within the first few weeks of the class to schedule brief, fifteen-minute office appointments with each of your students. While it is best to have a stock of work-oriented questions at hand (what are your expectations for this class? what are your ideas for the first paper? what have you thought of the first meetings or texts? how does this class relate to your future career interests?), these meetings are best conceived of as an opportunity to extend the personal introduction. This will make students feel both more comfortable and more *accountable*. If they feel like you have invested time in them, they will feel obliged to invest more time in the class and will do their best not to let you down.

Finally, I want to end with a word about endings. Skilled teachers know how to draw people out, and indeed can fill up with ease a seminar's allotted time with the language of excited students. The more experienced we are as teachers, the less time we need to spend preparing. The art of "winging it" is an essential survival skill for overburdened graduate students and junior faculty, but it can be taken too far. While one should of course always have the flexibility to allow students to surprise one and to take the conversation in unexpected and fruitful directions, it is also important to have an endpoint of some sort in mind for each class, an agenda which culminates in a moment of closure. It is often a good idea to be prepared in the last several minutes of class to give a mini-lecture developing an argument or theme which can tie together and summarize the discussion which has preceded it, as well as pointing to new and even counter-intuitive ideas which the students can take with them outside of the classroom. Often it is trepidation and insecurity which drives the novice to this extra effort. For the experienced teacher, it must be a matter of remembering the basics.

OVERLOOKED ESSENTIALS
FOR CLASSROOM DISCUSSIONS

MARY-ANN WINKELMES

A great deal of attention, in print and in practice, has been devoted to the process of leading discussions in college and university classrooms. Most writing on the subject consists of analyses of successes and failures, or techniques prescribed for making specific improvements.[1] This essay falls into neither category. Instead, it invites teachers and students at all levels of expertise to consider several essential but overlooked principles that are too often taken for granted. These are not teaching techniques, but rather fundamental considerations from which techniques might be derived: 1) the discussion group's dynamic, 2) its common goals, and 3) its control of both the content and the form of a discussion as it unfolds. The "voice" I use to describe these principles is informed by my own teaching experience and also by a chorus of other teachers who have generously shared their insights in discussions on pedagogy.

That these overlooked factors are concerned with "process" might at first draw skepticism from teachers who responsibly aim to convey to their students as much of the content of a discipline as possible. Indeed, when I taught a seminar on the methods of art history for the first time, my own desire to provide my students with important information about the methods and history of the discipline caused me to overlook the essentials I now recommend. I thought that spending class time on issues of process would distract my students from the subject matter of the course. By the end of that semester, both I and my students had learned that when the whole group examines and understands the processes used to study course content, the focus on that content grows sharper and more efficient. I credit my students for initiating that lesson. After I had spent weeks encouraging them to analyze past and present methods of practicing art history, they quite logically began to analyze our seminar group's methods of study as well. Once we had examined together the rationale for the course's organization, along with the benefits and drawbacks of certain patterns of discussion that had evolved in our group, my students' ability to sustain focused and productive two-hour discussions increased dramatically, as did their mastery of the course's content.

Group Dynamic

My first seminar students may have been exceptional in their commitment to learning about art history and in their cooperation with each other and me. Students and teachers at any college or university know that an ideal group dynamic for a discussion is attained only rarely. Teachers commonly worry that their class may fragment around an issue, that some students may become hostile when criticizing or defending ideas, and that others may not engage with the issues at all. Those who succeed in cultivating an atmosphere in which the teacher and students stimulate each other's thought in conversations that continue even outside the classroom are often disappointed when they cannot easily replicate that ideal using the same techniques in subsequent classes. This can confound teachers at all levels, from the most experienced senior professors to beginning graduate-student teaching assistants. Even the most tried and true techniques will never work consistently, since each class is a unique entity. Ingredients of past successes usually do not produce the same results in combination with different groups of students. In fact, a teacher's reliance on techniques that worked in the past can lead to failure when the teacher assumes an expected result and fails to monitor students' actual responses.

Fortunately, the elusive, ideal group dynamic teachers strive for is not a necessary prerequisite for worthwhile classroom discussions. The teacher who expects to attain the ideal is bound to be frustrated and less effective than a discussion leader who accepts that this is unlikely. In fact, explicit acknowledgment at the outset by teacher and students that a utopian class atmosphere is unnecessary can be a unifying premise for a discussion group. After that, the group can enumerate those elements that are absolutely essential to a productive discussion—and then discover that as a group of socialized human beings they can fulfill and even exceed those requirements.

For a worthwhile discussion to occur, class members need not know each other well or even like each other. They need only agree to be respectful of one another while the discussion is underway. For example, even those students who hold extreme beliefs can agree to hear opposing views when they know this is what insures the group's consideration of their own opinions. Virtually any group of students and their teacher, even a group of complete strangers at their very first meeting, can agree to acknowledge each person's comments and opinions with equal attention (before expressing agreement or disagreement) during class, thus making it possible for the group to progress toward the common benefit that a worthwhile discussion will provide. One teacher I know led a comparative religion seminar whose students included an agnostic ex-convict and a fundamentalist Christian. Not surprisingly, these two students sometimes expressed conflicting ideas vehemently. This teacher now invites her students in the first class meeting each semester to help her define specific ground rules for their discussions: how speakers are recognized, how evidence is used and evaluated, how ideological disagreements are negotiated, and how violations of the accepted modes of classroom discourse are handled. In my own seminar classes at the beginning of each semester, I explain that discussion in class should include thoughtful, focused listening to classmates' comments followed by direct responses, as opposed to a series of unrelated announcements by individuals anxious to make their own points.

Common Goals

Just as the protocols for discussion can be identified and agreed upon at the beginning of a semester, so the goals for each particular discussion can be enumerated at the beginning of each class meeting by teacher and students together. The teacher may identify a few key topics and then invite students to add related ones to the day's agenda. This enables everyone to be aware of all aspects of the agenda for the discussion. To allow for spontaneity, the agenda can include exploration of related but unforeseen ideas.

Too often in classroom discussions, some of the subject matter to be covered is part of a "hidden agenda" revealed by the teacher only as he or she manipulates the discussion. Yet a discussion more often succeeds in generating a mutual and satisfying consideration of ideas when all members know in advance the topics on the agenda. The act of jointly and explicitly enumerating the topics for discussion provides an initial incentive for the group to achieve its aims. Participants tend to feel a sense of mutual responsibility for the discussion that follows. Furthermore, students who hesitate to join in a class discussion because they are uncertain of the relevance of their comments are more likely to contribute when they can identify their ideas as related (directly or tangentially) to the defined agenda.

It wasn't until I began facilitating discussions on pedagogy for groups of graduate-student teaching fellows (whom I saw as somewhat less experienced peers) that I recognized the value of a jointly established discussion agenda. In this context, I understood each discussion as an exploration of ideas by colleagues, each of whom had an equal right to help define the agenda and to share responsibility for addressing it. The cooperation and commitment these teachers brought to our explorations of the shared agendas at first astonished me. Later, many told me they experienced an energy in our discussions that was absent from graduate seminars in their disciplines where they did not feel like junior colleagues of their teachers, but instead like less important and somewhat less respected apprentices. This inspired me to rethink my teaching of art history along similar lines. I tried applying the principle of common goals to my art history courses. Particularly in seminars, and to a limited degree in lectures, I invited students to join me in establishing the agenda for each day's meeting. I began thinking of my students as less experienced colleagues in our joint investigation of the discipline. This fundamental change has even increased my interest in teaching subject matter I have taught many times before. Each exploration of a subject begins with a slightly different agenda, and follows an individual path, based on each group's contributions. For me, this revelation came just at the time when I had begun to feel a generational distance from students. Reconfiguring class discussions as collegial explorations of a shared agenda allowed me to find common ground once again with my students.

Control of Process and Content

The goals enumerated by a class group at the outset of a discussion can include not only the topics to be addressed but also the process by which to pursue them. Just as the generally consistent aspects of this process are established at the beginning of a course (like the specific ground rules established by my colleague with the ex-convict and fundamentalist Christian in her seminar), so the more specific process goals (like monitoring of time allocation and of methodological approaches or disiplinary tools to be used) can be negotiated at the beginning of each discussion.

Teachers often reserve for themselves the responsibilities of identifying such process goals and leading the group to achieve them. Some may even fear that sharing this responsibility with students means relinquishing control of the discussion. Yet joint monitoring by the whole group of the process of a class discussion offers great benefits. A discussion can be more effectively focused when the teacher invites students to join him or her in guiding it. In addition, this method encourages an atmosphere in which students feel elevated to the status of junior colleagues, engaging with the teacher in a scholarly investigation, while at the same time following the teacher's model. For example, in my graduate art history seminars and in group discussions on pedagogy with teaching fellows, I invite participants to make the kind of comments they usually expect to hear only from the discussion leader. Such comments might include, "That's an important idea that leads us to the last big issue on our agenda. Let's come back to it after we've finished exploring the current item," or "We all agreed to devote half an hour to topic Y. We should wrap up topic X now—unless we prefer to adjust our plan," or "I'm not sure I understand how that idea connects with this topic—would you explain?" In this context, a student asking for further explanation is not only clearing up his or her own confusion, but also performing a valuable service for the whole group by sharpening the focus on content and clarifying the connections between topics on the agenda.

The teacher may even find it easier to consider productive but unforeseen ideas with students in a class discussion when he or she can rely on other members of the group to help assure that the discussion doesn't stray unproductively from its stated goals. When group members share responsibility for controlling both the content and the form of their discussions, it becomes easier for the group to achieve its jointly established goals.

Discussion groups benefit from considering the three principles recommended here because ground rules for modes of discourse in discussions, common goals for content, and the processes for monitoring adherence to those goals are most effective when they are designed by each group to suit its own needs. Deriving teaching and learning techniques in this way insures that no technique goes unexamined and that actual results are monitored and not just assumed. My own seminars on art history and discussion programs on pedagogy continue to affirm that calling a discussion group's attention to the three essentials examined here helps produce efficiently focused, collaborative explorations of issues by a teacher and his or her student colleagues.

TEACHING AND LEARNING
BEYOND THE CLASSROOM

GETTING THE MOST OUT OF WEEKLY ASSIGNMENTS: USING FEEDBACK AS A MOTIVATIONAL TOOL

SUJAY RAO

While researchers mention a multiplicity of factors that drive students, a substantial body of work now argues that active learning strategies in the classroom, when used well, help build motivation.[1] But little has been written about how these strategies can be reinforced outside the classroom in order to motivate students to the fullest. I will argue here that effective use of weekly or regular writing assignments can increase both the quantity and the quality of students' involvement with a course's subject matter.

Most basically, weekly or regular writing assignments ensure that students, juggling many commitments, are forced to do at least a percentage of the work for the course each week. That is to say, given an assignment that must be completed and that will count as part of their grade, most students will do the work required to complete the assignment. This guaranteed minimum engagement with the material in turn gives students a basic preparation for discussions in the classroom. The completed assignments themselves also prove useful to the instructors by providing glimpses of how individual students understand the course material at regular intervals throughout the term.

But the benefits of regular writing assignments such as short (one to two page) response papers are far greater than these. As Richard Light has shown in a study of Harvard undergraduates, students feel more personally engaged and challenged in courses with frequent writing assignments.[2] Some researchers claim that students are best motivated by material that lies just above their current level of understanding—material that provides a challenge, but not an impossible one.[3] It follows that regular writing assignments designed to encourage higher-level thinking (application, analysis, synthesis, evaluation) can encourage a challenging and satisfying engagement with course work.

Such assignments can also encourage students to make intellectual transitions. Research suggests that students pass through three fundamental but intellectual transitions: dualistic ("black-and-white") thinking giving way to an awareness of multiplicity; the transition from awareness of multiplicity to contextual relativism (the idea that there are some absolutes, for example in physical sciences, but that there are many unknowns); and the gradual development of commitments and beliefs (which may change over time) based on personal knowledge and experience.[4] Regular writing assignments building on basic factual knowledge and comprehension, but directed at higher-level skills, offer an ideal way to motivate students by challenging them to make an intellectual transition. For example, after students read a study of post-conquest Spanish-American societies, replete with information on social and economic changes, I instruct them, "Given what you know about colonial Spanish America, briefly evaluate the social and economic impact of the conquest." Such an assignment, while based on concrete facts, challenges students to formulate judgments about the material they have studied, while also developing skills of synthesis and evaluation. It also makes seemingly isolated facts more meaningful and more relevant for students by connecting them to larger issues. In short, this type of assignment can motivate students by offering an attainable challenge while also allowing them the satisfaction of answering a meaningful question.

An instructor's responses to students' papers can greatly reinforce—or damage—the motivational effect of this type of question. Few things can dampen students' enthusiasm quite as quickly as perfunctory praise ("Good job") or overly critical comments ("You obviously have not thought about…") from an instructor. On the other hand, as I found with my students in a Latin American history course, feedback that recognizes their efforts and provides specific suggestions for improvement can motivate students to work harder. Examples of my comments on some of their papers follow shortly.

Instructors can further help to build students' extrinsic motivation (which relies on rewards such as praise, good grades, acquisition of skills crucial for a particular career, or credit earned toward a degree) and, more importantly, their intrinsic motivation (which derives from interest in learning for its own sake) by keeping certain basic principles in mind.[5] First, recognize students' effort. "Mirroring" represents an effective technique for doing this.[6] "Mirroring" involves restating the argument of the paper so as to reassure the student that you have read the paper with interest and have understood the argument the student presents. (Example: "Michael, in this paper you have done a good job examining Richardson's use of archae-ological evidence to support his claims of changes in Roman society before the barbarian invasions. In particular, you make some interesting observations of a possible regional bias in this evidence.") Second, stress that what is good in students' papers comes not through genius, but through hard work. This is an important message both for students who lack confidence and believe that no amount of effort will save them from failure, and for students who believe that their innate intelligence allows them to work less than others. Offering specific and concrete strategies for improvement is one way of reinforcing the message that challenges can be overcome through effort.[7] Third, suggest how students might think further about the material, especially as it might tie in to larger issues of interest to them. Finally, to as great a degree as is possible, tailor feedback to the needs of individual students, in order to challenge them to reach the next stage in their intellectual development. To make all of this less abstract, I provide below sample responses to several possible scenarios arising from the above-mentioned question on the impact of the conquest on Spanish America.

One of my high-achieving students, María, writes an excellent two-page paper arguing that while the Spaniards brought new technologies to their colonies, they applied these technologies largely to activities such as silver mining which had little effect on daily life.[8] María also mentions that preliminary studies of skeletal remains suggest that the physical welfare of many Spanish Americans did not regain pre-Conquest levels until centuries later. María's paper shows an implicit awareness of arguments on both sides of the question, while it uses evidence to form and support her opinion on the matter; responding to it may seem to be a simple matter of praising her work. But I can also use this as an opportunity to reinforce intrinsic motivation. Engaging in a scholarly dialogue with her may be the best means of doing this. For example, I could ask María to think about regional differences in welfare, possible biases in the collection of skeletal evidence, and the extent to which the decline in welfare can be attributed to the behavior of the Spaniards rather than the spread of epidemic disease.

Another student, Norman, usually a high-achiever, turns in a disappointing paper, possibly the result of "slacking off." He argues that the impact of the conquest defies measurement. After all, he writes, the Spaniards ended human sacrifice and brought new technologies, such as iron tools, to the New World, but also wrought great destruction. Based on his previous work, I can tell that this essay derives more from a lack of thought about the material than from difficulty in forming a judgment. Frequently, students like Norman will be sensitive to others' opinions of their work. It may be enough for me to state that this paper, while acceptable, does not measure up to the high standard set by his previous work and to pose questions that Norman could have considered. For example, I could say to Norman:

> In this essay you have done a good job of identifying many of the changes accompanying the conquest and have noted the difficulties of measuring its multifaceted impact. However, this essay is not up to the high standard I have come to expect from your work. For instance, what practical effect did the new technologies introduced by the Spaniards have, and how widely were they adopted? Also, how much of the destruction accompanying the conquest was willful rather than attributable to epidemics?

Asking these questions identifies specific areas for improvement and lets Norman know that I expect high-quality work from him. Here, extrinsic motivation (mildly expressed criticism) represents a starting point for getting Norman involved with the material.

A third student, Alison, turns in a paper that demonstrates progress. Previously accustomed to making absolutist arguments, Alison now writes that while the conquest did initially bring violent destruction, the violence was temporary. Spanish rule, she argues, slowly incorporated the New World into a world economy that provided greater opportunities for economic growth. I take great care in responding to Alison's paper, seeing it as an opportunity to reinforce this breakthrough.

> Alison, your argument that the conquest brought greater economic opportunities for what became Spanish America is intriguing and subtle. This argument is made stronger by your acknowledgment and explanation of the initial violence of the conquest. Clearly, you have synthesized and carefully thought through a great deal of information presented in lectures and in the readings. You might also have considered the degree to which colonial rule continued to rely on violence or the extent to which the Crown allowed Spanish Americans to participate in the Atlantic economy.

Through these comments, I have rewarded Alison for her efforts, most notably her departure from an absolutist mindset. Alison still has much to learn about colonial Latin America, but the matter should not be pressed too hard at this point, for fear of discouraging her.

A fourth student, Jim, consistently turns in undistinguished papers, often riddled with factual errors. Motivating him through feedback is difficult, but not absolutely impossible. One option is to tell him, "Jim, this paper does an adequate job of considering some of the changes accompanying the conquest." The hope of clearer praise may offer some extrinsic motivation. I also imply that more effort would have paid off by stating, "The essay would have been stronger if you had considered the practical effect on everyday life of the technologies brought by the Spaniards." I choose not to dwell on Jim's factual errors in my comments. While I draw his attention to them by my comments in the margin of his paper, I feel that Jim will make little progress in comprehending the material until he cares about it. For this reason, I try to draw out interesting implications of the material in order to arouse Jim's interest. For example, I ask, "How significant is the study of skeletal remains? What, if anything, do these remains say about three centuries of colonial rule?" Scholarly dialogue may be the best means to motivate a student such as Jim.

Some students may initially resent the additional demand on their time posed by weekly or regular writing assignments. However, in the end, the vast majority of students express satisfaction and even gratitude.[9] Discussions in which they and their colleagues are prepared and knowledgeable thrill students. Furthermore, students often appreciate the opportunity to express their thoughts and receive feedback as they absorb and assimilate the material. For example, one study of undergraduates finds that most students want detailed feedback soon after they complete an assignment, while the work is still fresh in their minds.[10] Students may also want to be held to a high standard, although they also want opportunities to revise their work prior to being graded. Finally, students want frequent checks on their knowledge such as quizzes, brief papers, and oral exams so that they can revise and improve their work.[11] Weekly or regular writing assignments can satisfy at least two of these three desires. Despite occasional complaints, students know that frequent assignments and feedback help them to work and to learn.

It may be objected that responding to weekly assignments poses a burdensome addition to instructors' already packed schedules. There is some truth to this argument in the short run. But, with practice, responding to students' writing in ways that will motivate them to think more, and more deeply, about the material will almost become second nature. And the results will be worth the effort: fewer bored, or even embittered, students and more papers that are engaging and even thought-provoking. Teachers and students can only benefit.

Selected Bibliography

Brophy, Jere. "Conceptualizing Student Motivation." *Educational Psychologist* 18:3 (1983): 200–215.

———. "Synthesis of Research on Strategies for Motivating Students to Learn." *Educational Leadership* 45:1 (1987): 40–48.

Bushey, Barbara. "Writing Improvement in the Harvard Expository Writing Program: Policy Recommendations, Suggestions for Faculty, and Suggestions for Students." Report presented to President Derek Bok by the Harvard Assessment Seminars, 1991.

Light, Richard. "Explorations with Students and Faculty about Teaching, Learning, and Student Life: First Report." Report of the Harvard Assessment Seminars, 1990.

———. "Explorations with Students and Faculty about Teaching, Learning and Student Life: Second Report." Report of the Harvard Assessment Seminars, 1992.

Lowman, Joseph. "Promoting Motivation and Learning." *College Teaching* 38:4 (Fall 1990): 136–139.

Lucas, Ann F. "Using Psychological Models to Understand Student Motivation." *New Directions for Teaching and Learning* 42 (Summer 1990): 103–114.

Perry, William G. *Forms of Intellectual and Ethical Development in the College Years: A Scheme.* New York: Holt, Rinehart, and Winston, 1970.

Wlodkowski, *Motivation and Teaching.* Washington, D.C.: National Education Association, 1978.

HOW TO IMPROVE STUDENTS' WRITING BEFORE READING ANY

KERRY WALK

It can sometimes seem from the evidence—their essays—that students need to be tricked or cajoled into writing readable prose. Clearly they won't do so voluntarily, we reason, or the proof would be in their papers. As an Expository Writing teacher at Harvard University and a former live-in advisor at one of Harvard's undergraduate residential houses, I have read hundreds of student essays in fields as various as archaeology, history of science, folklore, psychology, political science, and African-American Studies. Until I spent time talking with students about their writing process, I wondered why they often write so disappointingly in the courses they take across the curriculum. I had assumed, as too many of us do, that disappointing student essays—unfocused, structurally flawed, plodding and dull, at times incomprehensible—are the impoverished brainchildren of indifference. Though this assumption is sometimes correct, I have found that students write more often in haste than indifference *per se*—haste that results in an overly compressed writing process and, inevitably, mediocre writing. How can you, their teacher, use your knowledge of their writing process to help students write better papers?[1] An answer to this question, as I will suggest, is *through the use of writing groups.*[2] More than any other pedagogical intervention I know of, writing groups give students a sense that they're writing for real readers; it also ultimately teaches self-critique, one of the hardest skills to learn and the one most necessary for revision.

When I teach writing skills, such as structuring an argument and using evidence, I deliberately slow students' writing process down: they do several pre-draft assignments aimed at focusing and developing ideas, produce a working draft that we meet to discuss, then revise the draft and submit it for evaluation. After I critique and grade it, students may choose to revise this "final" draft one more time. Read, think, plan, write, revise, revise again—the process has the advantage of producing some excellent writing, but for instructors who are not specifically teaching writing (and even for some who are), it is also prohibitively laborious and time-consuming. Students writing papers for courses in which the process is *not* broken down into discrete stages—that is, for most of their courses—may abbreviate this process or bypass some of its stages because of self-imposed time constraints. Indeed, the great majority of the hundred and fifty or so first-year students I recently surveyed report that they start only two days ahead when writing a five-to-seven-page paper; on the first day they plan, on the second they draft. Predictably, sophomores, juniors, and seniors, who tend to be involved in more pursuits outside the classroom than first-year students and who are also more confident in their ability to "get by" academically, spend even less time on papers, often starting the day, even the night, before the paper is due.

Dara, a junior, is typical. A gifted writer who describes herself as "anal" about her papers, she nevertheless admits that she spends much less time on the "shorter papers" now than she did as a first-year student. Now, instead of starting two days before the paper is due, she starts the night before: "I used to sit down and spill a lot of ink before I ever actually started writing the paper. If I was writing on a poem, I'd spend hours analyzing it, writing all over it, making notes in the margin. I really got to know that poem, and I could come up with something good to say about it. Now I start writing the draft too soon, before I've really done any prep work, and I write too fast to make it flow. Then, of course, I end up not having time to revise." Like many of the students I spoke with, Dara shortchanges all three main stages of the writing process—planning, drafting, and revising—because she doesn't take the time she needs. Another student, a junior named Mike, describes his experience in different terms but to the same effect: "I usually procrastinate until panic sets in, then I write furiously and revise once. I barely make the deadline." Many other students describe such ad hoc writing strategies as "sitting in front of the computer" and "staring at the monitor" until they "come up with an idea"; others, such as Lauren, a sophomore, write their papers "straight through, taking breaks for different reasons. I have no determined organization; I decide what each paragraph will be about when I get to it."

Each of these students lacks the deliberateness of Daniel, a first-year student. Like other students, Daniel "freaks out and procrastinates," but unlike others, he manages to spend sufficient time planning, drafting, and revising: "I work with the assignment and the texts until I can come up with an idea, then I collect quotes that I think will prove the thesis. I usually make a rough outline, maybe in my head or on paper depending on how complicated it is. Then I write a rough draft. After that, I get feedback from my TF [teaching fellow] and revise according to the feedback." Dara admits that a similar process worked for her in the days when she allotted more time to her writing tasks: "In Expos [Harvard's required first-year writing class], it was great, because I would be really ready to write a draft, and after I had one I would revise and revise and revise, and the paper would end up being really pretty good." Not surprisingly, for these and many other students, the chance to revise makes a significant difference in the quality of the final product. In a recent study of undergraduate writing, students reported that the single greatest help an instructor can give them as writers—more than handing out writing tips, providing model essays, or responding to paper ideas—is to discuss their drafts with them in conference and give them the opportunity to revise.[3]

"But I just don't have the patience to revise like that anymore. If it's not built into the course, I don't do it," says Dara. One simple way of building revision into your course when you aren't able to meet with every student to discuss drafts, or even when you are, is to organize students into writing groups of two or three people each; the students read each other's papers, respond either in person or in writing, and then revise. The use of writing groups, whether in a small seminar or large lecture course, invites students to negotiate their ideas with peers instead of an authority figure. Doing so enables students to take an active role in their learning; it encourages them to conceive their goal when they write a paper, not as "giving the teacher what he or she wants," but rather as engaging and persuading a wider, often more critical readership. (It's no coincidence that students typically write better drafts for classmates than for instructors.) Although students can't necessarily provide scholarly guidance (for example, the context for a debate or a list of relevant sources), they can learn to identify weaknesses in an argument and make concrete suggestions for revision, skills they can eventually apply to their own writing. Other advantages to writing groups, according to Anne Ruggles Gere, are that participants "develop more positive attitudes about writing...experience intellectual growth, including development of critical thinking skills...[and] increase their rhetorical skill, particularly their ability to conceptualize and address the needs of their audience."[4] The result is better writing. As one senior observes, "It helps a *lot* to write a draft and give it to someone to read. Your focus becomes a lot clearer after people comment on what works and what doesn't. The opportunity to talk about and hear other ideas relating to what you've written helps to broaden your own idea, incorporate some new, interesting twists, and have a better paper."

But what of the main objection to writing groups—namely, that they benefit only weak writers? It may be true that weak writers have more to gain from writing groups: the sometimes excellent writing of their peers can startle them into seeing, possibly for the first time, the deficiencies in their own writing; the feedback they get can bring about truly dramatic improvement; and the chance to work through their ideas with classmates can significantly deepen their understanding of the material. But strong writers, both those who write intuitively, with no real awareness of what makes a good argumentative essay work, and those who write by formula, stand to benefit greatly from writing groups. By articulating the strengths and weaknesses of their peers' essays—a high-level teaching skill—these writers can become more reflective about their own writing. Reflection will help them not only translate their success with the standard five-pager into success with the much more difficult twenty-five-pager but also see where they can take greater risks in their writing—where they can experiment with structure, for example, or secondary sources. Moreover, strong writers have never had a monopoly on perspicacious critique; weak writers are equally capable of learning to become perceptive critics of their classmates' work. As someone who never shared a paper with anyone but teachers until graduate school, I think strong writers also benefit from seeing their ideas enter the public domain, where readers other than teachers may challenge and evaluate their thinking. In fact, perhaps the most important lesson we can teach student writers, weak or strong, is that their ideas must ultimately be tested in this larger context—the world of ideas. As part of that testing, all student writers must learn to distinguish their ideas from those of others writing in the field, whether the field is composed of classmates or published scholars. If you worry that weak writers working in groups may be overly influenced by the ideas of their classmates, you can seize the occasion to teach proper attribution of sources: students can learn to cite their classmates in notes or an acknowledgment, thereby re-creating the ethos of the scholarly community at large. You can also design assignments to give students greater latitude in their choice of topic, making it less difficult for them to differentiate their ideas from their peers'.

Writing groups benefit all writers, but students unused to getting feedback from classmates may dismiss a teacher's casual suggestion that they exchange papers; for writing groups to succeed, the process of working together must be clearly defined, and participation in the groups required. This is how I do it. I decide who the members of each group will be, basing my decisions on any number of factors: where the students live (the closer the better), how vocal they are in discussion (I like to put quiet students together to bring them out), how well they write (sometimes I mix weak and strong writers; sometimes I don't), and so on. On the day the draft is due, students bring enough copies for their group and for me. Although I may not actually read this particular draft, I want to make sure each student has handed one in; I can dock the grades of those who haven't. I announce the groups at the end of class, students exchange their papers, and a member of each group volunteers to e-mail me once the group has met. In a variation on this theme, a colleague of mine instructs students to respond to their group's drafts over e-mail and to append copies of the correspondence to their final versions. I usually allot one week for groups to meet and discuss drafts, thus pushing back the final due date by a relatively short amount of time.

This is the no-frills version of writing groups, and it usually gets adequate but no-frills results: if students haven't been taught how to critique an academic essay thoughtfully and constructively, they usually don't do it well. Lacking experience, they may praise their classmates' work regardless of its quality or give bad advice (which, it should be noted, most students claim is easy to spot) or make picayune suggestions ("fix this comma here") instead of commenting on larger writing issues, like thesis and structure. But even if the feedback students receive from their group is not especially useful, they come away with two valuable door prizes from the experience of handing in a draft for someone else to read: time to revise, which they didn't have before, and the revolutionary idea—new to most undergraduates—that papers are written to be read. As one student put it, "Writing groups have helped, just in terms of having to get an actual readable 'working' draft done and thinking of having real people read it."

In an important study of revision practices, Nancy Sommers has demonstrated a significant difference in the way student and experienced adult writers revise: whereas student writers tinker with wording but leave the draft essentially unaltered, experienced adult writers focus on argument—the essay's overarching idea, structure, and use of evidence.' The "frills" version of writing groups would be a vehicle for teaching students to revise the way experienced adult writers do—globally first, locally later. A simple way to accomplish this goal is to ask students to do two things: first, to submit their draft with a cover letter in which they discuss the problems they're encountering in terms of argumentation, and, second, to answer specific questions about the drafts they read. I usually give students a "reader response sheet" on which I pose several leading questions whose aim is to get students thinking about papers in global terms. I choose from among the following questions (though I always ask the first two):

- What is the issue, problem, or question with which the writer has framed the essay? In other words, what are the writer's intellectual motives for writing this essay? How can these motives—the "so what?" of the essay—be brought out?
- What is or should be the essay's thesis, or main idea? (Mistrust the stated thesis if there is one.) Does the thesis have enough focus?
- What· is the structure, or organizational scheme, of the essay? Is it logical? Does it flow? Does the argument make sense?
- What counter-arguments or counter-examples does the writer need to consider?
- Where does the writer need to provide more evidence or develop the ideas further?
- What general suggestions can you make about style? Is the style appropriate for its audience?

Such questions guide readers'—and writers'—attention away from mechanics (the work of editing and polishing) and toward argumentation. They also help inculcate an important habit of mind: seeing things from an "outsider's perspective," to use one student's phrase. "I understand what I'm writing," this student says, "but that's not necessarily a guarantee that my reader will, so it's helpful to have a second take on the content and clarity of what I'm trying to say." Other students talk about the value of "a fresh perspective" and "an objective read." "It's very hard to step back from your own paper to see what needs work," one first-year student observes. "Often," says another, "I find out that ideas I thought I had made clear in the essay weren't actually that apparent." The process of learning to see their own work through others' eyes can have a significant impact on student writing: students essentially become better writers by becoming better readers.

When time permits, you can facilitate this crucial process by participating in the writing groups yourself and modeling collegial behavior for students.[6] In this deluxe version of writing groups, you can show students how someone in your discipline thinks about writing, one of the main intellectual activities of every academic field, and how colleagues critique one another's work. Participation, of course, requires that you read students' drafts and schedule meetings with each group. I run the meetings by asking the first volunteer to remind the group what his or her essay is about. (I find that it's usually the writer, not the readers, who needs reminding.) After explaining that members should address their remarks to the writer, I ask the group, "What do you think?" or "Where should we begin?" or "Do you think that description of the paper is accurate?" If we're focusing on a specific aspect of argumentation, I'll ask a question about that. The meeting takes off from there. I find that most of the points I want to make get covered by other people and, what's more, that students' explanations to each other are often more effective than mine; half my age, they speak one another's language—the language of "flow" and "creativity" and many other terms whose precise meanings I'm only beginning to understand.

I also find that in my company students are emboldened to look at global writing issues, such as thesis and structure, and to make suggestions for radical revision. I am ceaselessly surprised at how seriously students are willing to take their work; the excellent quality of their revisions proves just how seriously. But my main finding, and the reason I prefer group conferences to individual ones, is that group conferences to some extent even out the asymmetrical relationship between teacher and students, substituting the power of group consensus for the power of teacherly authority. Neither adversary ("she just didn't agree with my opinion") nor oppressor ("he only likes my papers when I give him exactly what he wants"), the "teacher" becomes merely the most experienced reader in a group of readers, the first among peers. This is a model of education that, in my experience, is fulfilling for teacher and student alike. If you can't or don't want to meet with all of your students in small groups, you can achieve a similar, though diminished, effect by holding an in-class draft workshop—an examination of one or two drafts (or parts of drafts) by the class as a whole.[7]

Although students undoubtedly benefit more from meeting in small writing groups with an instructor who has read everyone's paper and can personally attend to each draft's particular strengths and weaknesses, the in-class draft workshop has the advantage of conserving time and effort while still having a sizable pay-off. I prepare for a workshop by asking students to read a draft or two before class and respond in letters addressed to the writer in which they focus on specific aspects of the draft, such as whether or not the thesis is developed logically. In class, I hold a discussion in which I help students identify problems and make concrete suggestions for improvement. At the end of the discussion, I generalize the lesson, making it clear how the discussion is relevant, not just to the person on the hotseat, but to every student in the classroom. For example, I might note that, like most of the students' drafts, this one has an unfocused thesis or only superficial analysis of evidence, and that everyone should take to heart the suggestions given to the draft writer. If you don't make this crucial pedagogical move, students may walk away from the workshop believing that one or two students got all the help while everyone else got nothing; by generalizing, you can show students how the workshop was relevant to everyone. In a variation of a draft workshop, I workshop excerpts from drafts—an introduction or conclusion (or both together), an analysis of a piece of evidence, the integration of a secondary source, and so on—which I sometimes hand out on the spot. Whether you workshop whole drafts or tiny excerpts, you'll be teaching students to think about the elements that make up a good essay as well as how to be better critics—first of others' work, then of their own.

Like me, you probably rely on readers' responses to your written work. By the time this article goes to press, it will have been read by several friends and colleagues, some of the students whose words I quote, the editor of this volume, and my mother.[8] I will have revised countless times in response to their suggestions and explored many of the avenues their comments opened up to me. This piece will, I trust, be better for having been read and critiqued by others, both practitioners of my discipline and more general readers with an interest in pedagogy. My commentators will have helped me sharpen my ideas and present them coherently, and challenged me with new ideas. Writing groups in courses give students a similar opportunity: the chance to practice an academic discipline actively and responsibly through engaged conversation with colleagues—the chance, that is, to behave like scholars.

Selected Bibliography

Bell-Metereau, Rebecca. "Breaking Boundaries, Solving Problems, Giving Gifts: Student Empowerment in Small Group Work." In *Writing With: New Directions in Collaborative Teaching*, pp. 247–64. Edited by Sally Barr Reagan, Thomas Fox, and David Bleich. Albany: State University of New York Press, 1994.

Elbow, Peter. *Writing without Teachers*. New York: Oxford University Press, 1973.

Gere, Anne Ruggles. Writing Groups: *History, Theory, and Implications*. Carbondale and Edwardsville: Southern Illinois University Press, 1987.

Harvey, Gordon. "Asking for It: Imagining the Role of Student Writing." *ADE Bulletin* 116 (Spring 1997): 3–7.

Rodburg, Maxine. "Workshops in the Teaching of Writing." In *How Writers Teach Writing*, pp. 143–56. Edited by Nancy Kline. Englewood Cliffs, NJ: Prentice Hall, Inc., 1992.

Sommers, Nancy. "Revision Strategies of Student Writers and Experienced Adult Writers." In *The Writing Teacher's Sourcebook*, pp. 119–27. 2nd ed. Edited by Gary Tate and Edward P. J. Corbett. New York: Oxford University Press, 1988.

——— . *A Study of Undergraduate Writing at Harvard*. Cambridge: Expository Writing Program, Harvard University, 1994.

——— and Donald McQuade, eds. "Peer Editors at Work." In *Student Writers at Work: The Bedford Prizes, Second Series*, pp. 341–422. Boston: St. Martin's Press, 1986.

Whitman, Neal A. *Peer Teaching: To Teach Is to Learn Twice*. ASHE-ERIC Higher Education Report No. 4. College Station, TX: Association for the Study of Higher Education, 1988.

Making Grades Mean More
and Less with Your Students

JUDITH RICHARDSON

"**G**reat teacher, hard grader."
These were the words one of my students used to describe me last year on a teaching evaluation. At the time, I was a teaching assistant for a history course, and my duties included grading and leading weekly small group discussions designed to complement a large lecture course. I was really pleased to see that my hard work at teaching was appreciated. I was surprised, however, to see the words "hard grader" included in the appraisal. My surprise grew when I saw similar assessments on other evaluations. I had never thought of myself as a hard grader. I never wanted to be a hard grader. If I rarely gave out straight As, I also was conservative in dishing out Cs, and I had never assigned a failing grade. The student's assessment caused me to think about my grading, not only whether it was unusually harsh, but also how, either despite it or because of it, I could be thought of as a "great teacher."

Facing the Demons of Grading and Grade Inflation

Early on in my teaching career, when I was fretting over how to grade "correctly," a colleague advised, "Make it easy on yourself—make four piles: A, A-, B+, B. Easy." Certainly, it would be difficult not to be thought of as a hard grader with this grading plan. In 1992, approximately 91 percent of undergraduate grades at Harvard were B- or higher, while the grade of C, writes Craig Lambert in *Harvard Magazine*, "which nominally signifies an 'average' performance, [had] virtually disappeared from Harvard transcripts."[1] Such grade inflation is not limited to Harvard. In fact, grades have gone up at virtually every academic institution in the past 25 years.[2] As long as students see grades not only as determining prospects for employment or continued study, but also as indicators of personal worth, they more than want good grades; they expect them, need them, are desperate for them. As one teacher quoted in *Harvard Magazine* says, "the intensity of the pressure is such that students sometimes shed tears of grief on learning that they have received a B+."[3] I have had students complain about A–s.

Yet, while students continue to press for higher grades, there is substantial opposition to grade inflation, especially from professors and administrators. Arguments against grade inflation range from the belief that students benefit from a broader range of grades, to the idea that the broader social function of higher education involves sorting and ranking, and that giving out too many high grades is, therefore, unethical.[4] Beyond the theoretical debates, meanwhile, there are lurking issues of professional position and reputation. Students are apt to give better evaluations to more lenient graders.[5] Yet, teachers who give too many high grades risk being seen as pandering to students, and as Eleanor Agnew writes, "[a]lleged grade inflation may be a contributing factor in denial of promotion or even in dismissal" of teachers.[6]

Instructors, graders, and graduate-student teaching assistants occupy an often treacherous middle ground between professors looking to deflate grades and students in pursuit of high grade point averages. They must navigate between these apparently opposing commitments, while trying to preserve our prospects and our self-esteem.

Getting Past the Demons

As a graduate-student instructor, I realize that, for all my fretting over grades and for all the debates over grade inflation, there isn't much I or my peers can do about the macro-issues of grading, either in terms of eliminating grades, or of single-handedly taking on grade inflation. Nevertheless, my students' comments made me think about my grading standards, and then more basically about how I thought grades work or could work. Did I think grades were valuable? Yes. How were they valuable? Well, they could give a shorthand indication of work to be done, of things accomplished, or of the need for a meeting, sometimes. They could act as milestones on a path toward improvement, and as motivators, positive and negative. Yes, there was value in these letters. But really this was just part of the answer. If the letters were a shorthand, what were they shorthand for? And how could one keep them from looming too large in the minds of students and teachers alike? Christopher M. Jedrey writes in *The Art and Craft of Teaching*, "we can reduce the amount of unnecessary pain caused by grading and increase its usefulness to the students by thinking about how and why we grade."[7] In addition, we can express this thinking about grades in practices and policies that will "tame" grades and make them work as learning tools. What follows here are ideas on how to make grades mean both more and less to students—ideas which rest overall on making grades seem less a final judgment and more a part of a scholarly conversation.

Setting Guidelines, Criteria, and Limits

An important first step, I think, in beating back the demons of grading involves acknowledging that grading standards are subjective, not absolute. Instead of trying to find an objectively correct way to grade, what seems key to me is developing a consistent internal grading logic. Criteria for grading should be made clear at the beginning of a course, not only in delineating how much various assignments will be weighted in the final grade, but also in delineating what constitutes an A paper or exam, versus a B, C, or D.[8] Even though it is impossible to avoid subjectivity in grading, guidelines give both teacher and student a sense of what is expected, and help stabilize the shorthand meaning of individual grades within the boundaries of a particular class. (Also, distributed criteria can be referred to should a student show up grumbling about a grade.) More generally, I think it's important to be open and straight with students about the way you think about grading, and the way you think about teaching. Students should feel that the classroom is a safe place for them to think and experiment with ideas. Delineating the place and purpose of grades, and demystifying them, can help to free the classroom and to create a sense of broader purpose.

Comments as Conversation

One of the best opportunities to make grades meaningful, and to mitigate their potentially harsh impact, is through written comments. Grades on assignments reflect the degree of skill students show in communicating ideas, and grading does involve assessment of thought and content. In making comments, a teacher has to take on the task of pointing out problems which are reflected in a student's grade. However, comments also need to rise above the act of simply correcting or accounting.

Commentary, at the end of an assignment or paper and in the margins, should engage the student at the level of ideas, even if just to point out the promise of a good idea that could be better developed. It helps to consider assignments as part of a conversation in which the teacher responds to the subject or purpose, not simply the mechanics and details. At times it may be challenging to find an idea worthy of discussion in a student's work, but it is vital to take students' ideas seriously.[9] It can also be helpful to make reference to a student's performance in other aspects of the course— particularly class participation. A teacher can bolster a student's confidence, or relieve his/her distress over a less-than-desired grade if the teacher is encouraging about the student's participation in class. (Alternately, teachers may be able to draw out shy students by asking them to share in class the good ideas they demonstrate in their writing.) Overall, comments provide a place to let students know that you appreciate their thought and potential, and that a single grade is not the final judgment of their abilities.

Self-evaluation and Student Empowerment

Through teaching (and having been a student for a long time), I have come to believe that it is very important to allow students to "save face" by letting a teacher know when they could have done better work on a particular assignment, and to separate themselves from individual assignments and grades. This does not mean that each assignment should be accompanied by disclaimers and excuses. But there are ways to give students the sense that it is within their ability to assess their work *as* work, and to learn from the mistakes and successes of each project.

A good deal has been written recently about giving students a greater sense of empowerment in their own work and involving students in the process of evaluation.[10] One trick that I learned from another teaching fellow in history was to ask students to write on the back of their essays what main idea they wanted to convey in the essay, what they would have liked to have done better, or would change if they had the time, and what they would like to ask the teacher about their essay. In this way, students felt allowed to admit that their work might not be perfect, that they were working under time limits, and that they were aware of ways in which they could develop their work further. Opportunities for rewriting can similarly emphasize writing as a process and a conversation—the assignment as a learning tool, rather than a proof. Even if a teacher cannot allow students to help determine their own grades, he or she can give them an opportunity to voice their concerns about their work, and to treat their work as "in progress" whether or not they ever come back to the particular topic.

Beyond Grading: Closing Thoughts

Certainly, students' quality of expression affects teachers' ability to grasp their ideas, and a student's work affects a teacher's perception of the person who turns it in. Ultimately, though, the suggestions presented here, and the broader idea of conversing through grades, rest on two key concepts. The first, reflected in the multidimensional approaches to commenting and evaluation discussed above, is that although skills and ideas are related, there are differences between them. The second, which has less to do with actual practices of grading, but is nonetheless important for the success of grading and class dynamics, is simply that students are people. Whether a teacher invites students to appointments at the beginning of the semester, or simply acknowledges them in class, a teacher's demonstrated awareness of students' outside activities and concerns allows students to feel that the teacher understands the pressures that affect their performance. In my experience, such recognition helps to alleviate the weight of grades in students' evaluations of themselves and their teachers, and at the same time, to transform grades into more useful educational tools. Even in an atmosphere of grade inflation, a "hard grader" who strives to converse through and beyond the grades, can be perceived by students as a "good teacher."

80 RICHARDSON

Selected Bibliography

Agnew, Eleanor. "Departmental Grade Quotas: The Silent Saboteur." Paper presented at the 44th Annual Meeting of the Conference on College Composition and Communication, San Diego, California, 31 March –3 April 1993.

Braxton, John M. et al. "Anticipatory Socialization of Undergraduate College Teaching Norms by Entering Teaching Assistants." *Research in Higher Education* 36 (December 1995): 671–86.

Dey, Eric L., et al. "Does Being Student-Centered Lead to Academic Standards? Faculty Orientations and Grading Practices." Paper presented at the 35th Annual Forum of the Association for Institutional Research, Boston, Massachusetts, 28–31 May 1995.

Guskey, Thomas R. "Making the Grade: What Benefits Students?" *Educational Leadership* 52 (October 1994): 14–20.

Guzzio, Tracie Church. "Collaborative Conclusions: Involving Students in the Evaluation Process." Paper presented at the 47th Annual Meeting of the Conference on College Composition and Communications, Milwaukee, Wisconsin, 27–30 March 1996.

"Involving Students in Evaluation." *English Journal* 78 (November 1989): 75–77.

Jedrey, Christopher M. "Grading and Evaluation." in *The Art and Craft of Teaching*, pp. 103–115. Edited by Margaret Morganroth Gullette. Cambridge, Massachusetts: Harvard-Danforth Center for Teaching and Learning, 1984.

Lambert, Craig. "Desperately Seeking Summa." *Harvard Magazine*, May-June 1993, pp. 36–40.

Larson, Laura. "Making Writing Real: 'Rewrite Days' and Other Empowerments." College Teaching 43 (Fall 1995): 132–33.

Nimmer, James G. "Effects of Grading Practices and Time of Rating on Student Ratings of Faculty Performance and Student Learning." *Research in Higher Education* 32 (April 1991): 195–215.

Placier, Margaret. "'But I Have to Have an A': Probing the Cultural Meanings and Ethical Dilemmas of Grades in Teacher Education." Paper presented at the Annual Meeting of the American Educational Research Association, Atlanta, Georgia, 12–16 April 1993.

LESSONS FROM MICHELANGELO AND FREUD ON TEACHING QUANTITATIVE COURSES

TODD BODNER

What do Michelangelo and Sigmund Freud have to do with improving instruction in sections (weekly, small-group class meetings designed to complement lectures) of quantitative courses? Michelangelo painted a monumental ceiling, one detail at a time, always keeping the larger whole in mind. The big picture perspective is an important facet of successful teaching in quantitative courses. Sigmund Freud wrote about conflicting psychic forces which are similar to the conflicting forces facing an instructor when it comes time to grade and comment on students' written work.

The Big Picture

In most courses, it is not uncommon for students to get mired in the details and miss the larger themes. If asked what they learned in a particular course, students are likely to focus on the particular techniques they learned instead of the larger, unifying concepts. Students may do well on problem sets where mathematical calculation is the primary focus, but poorly on their exams or term papers, where they must choose the best technique for addressing a particular question. Students should be encouraged to step back from the details and to view the whole picture, just as Michelangelo must have climbed down from the scaffolding where he worked to view the entire Sistine Ceiling now and again.

Experimental research in psychology has confirmed the big picture approach by demonstrating that memory for details increases when they are considered with the larger whole in mind. Research subjects were presented with a one-paragraph description of the actions involved in washing clothes by hand. Half of them were told in advance that the paragraph was about the washing of clothes and half were not. The participants who were informed of the context prior to reading the paragraph remembered many more of the details than those who read the same description without first knowing the overall context.[1] I have found two particular strategies useful in my students' awareness of the big picture in statistics courses. These techniques focus on 1) making sure the students know the aims of the course and 2) framing each lesson with the overall course goals, previous lessons, and the lessons soon to come.

Why is it necessary to study statistics? I pose this question to my students each year to clarify the purpose of the course. In leading the discussion, I try to draw out the students' motives and the rationale offered by their respective academic disciplines. I write these on the board. My goal is for the students to realize that statistical methods are simply another tool they can use to construct an argument. I explain that in high school, students are taught how to make verbal and written arguments for or against an idea. Statistical methods, I continue, are used for exactly the same purpose. It is the aim of a statistics course to introduce students to this new set of tools for making arguments. After this discussion, I pass out a few examples of how statistical methods are used in various academic disciplines. Short research reports from publications such as *Science* and *Nature* are ideal for this. In these research reports, I highlight both the scientific question the authors pose and the corresponding statistical method that they use to answer it. After some discussion, students realize that before long they will have the ability to interpret these same numbers and make similar statistical statements in support of an argument.

The sheer number and variety of statistical techniques to which students are exposed in an introductory course can be overwhelming. In order to make the material more manageable, I spend the first and last few minutes of each class connecting that day's lesson with the overall course goals, past lessons, and lessons soon to come. The following is an example of a comment I made in the first few minutes of a recent class:

> We've discussed numerical procedures for summarizing data for the univariate case. Let's list them. We've discussed graphical procedures for summarizing data in the univariate case. Let's list them. Already these are powerful techniques we can

use to understand the nature of some phenomena and answer some research question.

Now we turn to a bit more complicated case, involving two variables at the same time. We call this the bivariate case. Again, remember our goal: to summarize a set of data so we can answer a research question we have. In the bivariate case we have numerical procedures and graphical procedures to summarize our data set, just like in the univariate case. Today we will focus on these procedures. Adding these procedures to our statistical toolbox has given us a level of explanatory power that is a giant leap from our explanatory power the univariate case gave us.

This continues to be the case when we move beyond the bivariate case. Each additional added variable makes our explanatory power increase tremendously. But with each added variable, the ease with which we can use graphical procedures and numerical methods as summaries becomes more complicated. Let's make sure we understand the summarization of a data set in this bivariate case. We'll consider what we call the multivariate case later in the semester.

In every class, I devote the last few minutes to topics that we soon will consider in the course. The important elements of a teacher's concluding statement to the class include summaries of that day's lesson, the next topic that will be covered, and how both topics relate to the overall course goals. This triple focus helps students to prepare themselves for the upcoming material. The following are some concluding comments I made in a recent class:

We will finish up on descriptive statistics in the bivariate case very quickly. From there we will move on to the concept of probability and will explore some different types of distributions (recall what distributions are). Why is the study of probability important? Up to this point we have considered only what we call descriptive statistics, graphical and numerical summaries of a particular data set. But often we want to generalize our summary statistics beyond the given data set. Introducing probability concepts gives us a formal way to talk about these issues of generalizing findings. So while you may get bored with the examples of flipping coins and rolling dice, remember that the concepts surrounding probability will be used in a more meaningful domain, the research that you and I might conduct to find out more about our world.

The Id, the Ego, and the Superego of Grading Problem Sets

An ability like Freud's to balance the conflicting motivations and forces of the psyche can help us to guide students outside the classroom context, when we grade their problem sets. The mind, according to Freud, consists of three interrelated structures—the id, the ego, and the superego—which coexist in constant, dynamic tension. Freud's id represents our basic instincts, what we *want* to do in the absence of any constraint. Few instructors relish grading. The id doesn't want to grade at all. Freud's superego represents the standards and rules of society, what we *should* do. The superego encourages us to provide constructive comments while grading, in order to further students' learning. Stuck in the middle of these three forces is the ego. Freud's ego tries to appease the id and superego while at the same time facing up to reality. The instructor's ego must do the same.

In developing my own grading ego, I have learned to grade more efficiently and to comment more effectively. First, I grade only a few problems at a time. Instead of grading all of student A's problems, then student B's problems, and so forth, I grade problems 1 and 2 for everyone, then grade problems 3 and 4 for everyone, etc. For a particular problem set, four or five questions at a time might be effective and for other problem sets one at a time might be more appropriate. The idea is to grade the problems in manageable blocks. This is efficient for a variety of reasons. If you are working from a grading key, you need only refer to it a few times until you've memorized the correct solutions to the problems in each block. I find that if my blocks are too big, I refer to these solutions much too often, wasting precious time. This method also makes grading more fair. A grader is likely to use a uniform standard using this technique. Most importantly, by seeing how all your students answer a particular problem, you can easily identify patterns of common misconceptions and errors.

Seeing students' misconceptions this way enables you to comment on their problem sets both efficiently and effectively. Students often want to know *why* they missed a problem rather than just that their answer was incorrect. One way to accomplish this is to write one explanation that addresses all of the misconceptions, rather than numerous individual explanations, and distribute it to the entire class. When I grade problem sets, I do so next to my computer. Whenever I come across a mistake, I write it down with the correct solution. I then send the comments in the word processing document out via electronic mail. If there are pencil and paper portions to my comments, I distribute them in the next class meeting. Because each new lesson builds on prior lessons, it is essential to distribute comments quickly. Here is an example of a comment I made on a problem recently:

> We have a couple of equations that are useful for finding the needed sample size for different kinds of studies. There was some confusion this week in which equation should be used when. Everyone who made mistakes on this problem used the equation on page 583 of the textbook when they should have used the equation on page 438. The equation on page 583 is useful when you are conducting a study where you are interested in estimating a proportion in some population. The equation on page 438 is useful when you are conducting a study where you are interested in estimating the average of some population. Spend a little time comparing the two equations and the examples in the book where the two equations are used. That should clear up the confusion.

This helps students learn *why* they missed a problem. Just as important, students who solved the problem learn common pitfalls that might snare them on the next problem set or on an examination. Finally, storing such comments on your computer (and back-up disks) improves your teaching in subsequent years. You will have a record of what issues confuse students and common mistakes they make in those situations. This is valuable information for you, your colleagues, and your future students.

It is easy for students to get lost in the details in a quantitative course. To create a sense of the big picture, I have found it useful to (1) make sure the students know the overall aims of the course and (2) spend a few minutes in each class framing each lesson with the overall course goals, previous lessons, and the lessons to come. To negotiate the many motives present when grading, I have found it useful to grade smarter, not faster. This means that I grade questions in manageable blocks and use handouts and mass electronic mailings to save time when commenting on mistakes.

CREATING THE ENVIRONMENT FOR BETTER STUDENT-TEACHER CONFERENCES

S tudent-teacher conferences can be the most difficult and frustrating part of teaching college, but they also contain the potential to be the most rewarding moments of our lives as teachers.[1] This chapter addresses not the difficult cases in which boundaries between teaching and other activities (such as counseling, courtship, and coercion) get crossed, but instead focuses on the ordinary meetings that we may require or our students may seek. In this, my approach follows that of Richard L. Baker, who writes: "Others lay down a set of rules to insure minimal moral competence. In contrast, my approach will be to hold up models of ethical excellence."[2] Baker uses May Sarton's novel *The Small Room* as a model through which to construct an expanded definition of the student-teacher relationship as a friendship based on "mediated intimacy." I have relied on my own experiences to elaborate how this might work, not just for our best students or the ones who are most like us, but for any student. Focusing on ethical excellence, my question is at once idealistic and practical: how can we best create the conditions for intellectually and emotionally satisfying student conferences?

Students come to their teachers for three basic reasons: to fulfill a course requirement, to seek extra help, or to share an enthusiasm. Many courses require at least one student-teacher conference, usually either at the beginning of term or the planning stages of a final project. My expository writing class includes four such conferences—one for each draft. These meetings work best when their goal is clear: did the student understand my comments on her writing? does she have questions about how to find sources? Since these are meetings are rituals, I often tell my class: "The first question I will ask you in conference is: 'What is your plan for revising this paper?'" and, when they come to my office, I am just as predictable as promised. As a result, less-prepared or shy students are less anxious—my dogged predictability is reassuring—even if they still don't have a plan, while more confident students, who may see this predictability ironically, are glad of the chance to dive into their ideas.

Most of the time, students respond to the question with a version of "I'm going to do what you said." Often, what I have pinpointed as the piece's major weakness corresponds to the section that the student was least happy with. Even this passive assent creates an opportunity to focus our attention on how to address the paper's weaknesses. With some frequency, students will come in with a plan that sounds likely to throw them off track or to address only trivial problems: "Well, it definitely needs a title and I'll be sure to spell-check," or "my roommate says before I get into the argument, I need to explain what the Civil War was." In these cases, I gently disagree, suggesting that the student's plan is not appropriate to the assignment or does not solve the main task of revision. Finally, the strongest—most confident or most talented—students will come with their own plan, be it a new outline or a reassertion of their intentions (for they feel themselves misunderstood). In these cases, of course, it is not difficult to respond to their developing ideas.

By focusing on the ritual aspect of a required student-teacher conferences, I can meet the technical goal of the conference within a few minutes and then let a student go if that is her desire. This does not mean being impatient, abrupt, or betraying fatigue. But it means that sometimes the conversation is simply over, and there is no need to force the student to remain in the office for a chat. Similarly, when a student comes to a meeting without having thought about the material at all, the conversation dies of its own accord and I can send her home to do more thinking. This requires judgment, but usually a few further questions clarify the matter. If a student does not have a plan for revising her draft, I will return to my written comments and suggestions. Which would she like to discuss further? Does she know how she plans to address the problem I've identified? If at this point, she is not merely undecided but indifferent, if she says—as a student did last week—"to be honest with you, I haven't really thought about it," she is free to go.

Many students seek out a teacher for extra help, and teachers can do a lot to alleviate the frustration of these meetings. As tourists, we learn that the Roman will not understand if we just speak English a little louder; likewise, if a student did not understand our first explanation, she may not understand its repetition. So, I seek new ways to explain the same point, often consulting my bookshelves for words (or a picture or a diagram) from someone else. When it's a grammatical or historical point, I will consult a reference book. For less definite questions, I root around more freely. Thus, if a student is struggling to write smart, concise, and lively conclusions, I might show her the last paragraph of an essay by a novelist, a scholar, and a journalist. Together, on the spot, we discuss what works in each case until the student begins to develop her own sense of the array of solutions other writers use, and thus may begin to find one or two with which she might be comfortable. By not being proud about my own ability to explain, by acknowledging that others explain the same thing differently, I help students move from embarrassment at being "behind" to the openness they need to learn. Furthermore, the book allows us to triangulate. The confusion no longer lies somewhere between my incompetence to explain and the student's failure to understand. Instead, the question becomes a recognition of complexity: this point is confusing, and, by extension, the student is right to question it. And from this questioning, we can determine the elements of her ideas, take them apart and rebuild them into an improved sentence.

While others' explanations can help improve a student's understanding of complicated concepts, our own efforts to explain or restate a student's ideas can be equally useful. What is this student trying to say? I take notes, silently improving minor errors, discussing the major ones. I use scrap paper to draw pictures and diagrams. Sometimes, it's just a matter of dividing a sentence or an argument into two sides, pro and con, but often the structure is more involved than that. I use metaphors. An argument can be like a switchback, a spiral, a pyramid, or a journey; it can take a left turn in the middle, build on the work of those who've come before, or end with a whimper. I encourage her to take notes, just as I am doing.

When students consult us for extra help, we often aim not to overwhelm them with too much information or direction. However, students may want to be given more direction than we suspect. Kathryn Evans describes a conference that the student judged to be a success. The student's ideas had been questioned, challenged, and interrupted; however, the young teacher, thinking she had been too didactic, assessed that same conference as unsuccessful. "In this case," Evans writes, "the teacher had an accidental hit; she helped the student."[3] But, as Evans notes, an "accidental hit" isn't excellent teaching. What this well-intentioned teacher overlooked is that her practice of letting the student direct the conference was resulting in conferences that the student characterized as "somewhat boring."[4] A difficult balance must be struck between giving the student so much information that she feels bullied, and withholding information so that the student leaves the conference without having learned anything new.

Most of us achieve that balance naturally when students arrive at our office not for a required conference or to seek extra help but to discuss their interest in an idea or a book. At such a moment, we delight in sharing our own enthusiasm, we accept the student's desire for communion, and we may openly and willingly share extra information—the kind that won't be on the test but that illuminates and expands the course's focus. These are the meetings I remember most fondly from my years as a student: the time I was given a copy of *What Maisie Knew* because my professor thought I needed to read it, the time a professor from whom I'd never taken a course stopped me to ask about my senior thesis. True, these were English professors, and I went on to graduate school in English. Not all of our students are like us (thank goodness!), but, like us, they seek some communion with a mentor, a desire which is "neither inappropriate nor importunate."[5] If we truly aim at ethical excellence, then we should assume each conference has the potential to be an intellectually exciting event. This means that our most motivated students are not the only ones with whom we are unguarded, exploratory, witty, or helpful with extra sources. Less motivated students especially stand to benefit from the experience of watching us think and witnessing our enthusiasm.

In "Good Talk about Good Teaching," Parker Palmer discusses the metaphors we use to describe our job to ourselves. I've compared my own teaching to that of a coach and a judge, but my best teaching comes from my idea of myself as a person who reads and thinks in front of students. These moments sometimes occur in the classroom, but they happen more frequently and more naturally in my office. And, if I'm in a proper office with books on the shelves, I can turn to a reference book, an anthology, to something I have just been reading, and share that with the student. These moments work—that is, they lead to more interesting discussions and, eventually better papers and more thoughtful students—precisely because I often fumble. Through my own searches they see how meandering and accidental my own connections can sometimes be. As I search my mind and my shelves, we talk about what it is I hope to find, and why I think this student may be interested in something that has interested me. I let them see me thinking in the hopes this helps them make connections among the books they're reading, and between that reading and their own experience. When students are anxious, such moments provide a welcome pause in which they can collect their thoughts and witness the fact that, though I am the teacher, I am often uncollected. If nothing pertinent is ready to hand, we can rethink the parameters of our search, the demands of the assignment. By modeling and recommending what to do in their situation, we show that we take our students seriously; we assume that they have independent minds and show them that we expect them to behave accordingly.

Conducting the kind of fruitful conferences I'm describing here depends on having a proper office with bookshelves, something many teaching fellows, adjunct and junior faculty may not have. That many of us conduct conferences in coffee shops, communal office spaces, or library lounges accounts for some of the frustration of student-teacher conferences. Outside of an office—however humble—it is difficult to model for students how we would go about solving the problems that they are struggling with. Our institutions can help us create the possibility of successful conferences, satisfying to both teacher and student, by finding creative ways to offer all teachers access to office space.

Taking an interest in student-teacher conferences means acknowledging the extent to which our teaching creates relationships with students, and the extent to which students want to see us as thinking people. As Richard Baker writes, "This does not mean…that the professor…'hangs out' with students. It does mean, however, that the professor brings passion to her subject, and gives of herself for the students' good. With such passionate self-giving, the professor acts as a friend to the students through the medium of the subject matter."[6] Such connection is possible in all student-teacher conferences, especially if the purpose is clear, books and resources are near to hand, and our instruction is engaged and resourceful.

Selected Bibliography

Baker, Richard L., Jr. "The Ethics of Student-Faculty Friendships." *New Directions for Teaching and Learning* 66 (Summer 1996): 25–32.

Evans, Kathryn. "'That's Not What I Meant': Failures of Interpretation in the Writing Conference." Bethesda, MD: ERIC Document Reproduction Service, ED 375 399. 1994

Hacker, Tim. *Teacher Conferences as a Modeling Technique for Peer Response.* Bethesda, MD: ERIC Document Reproduction Service, ED 372 404. 1994.

Hull, Glynda. *'This Wooden Shack Place': The Logic of an Unconventional Reading. Occasional Paper No. 22.* Bethesda, MD: ERIC Document Reproduction Service, ED 335 679. 1990.

Lefavor, Ann Oury. *Motivating Students to Change: Intensive Short Term Counseling Techniques Enhance Teaching of Composition.* Bethesda, MD: ERIC Document Reproduction Service, ED 384 039. 1995

Murray, Harry, et al. "Ethical Principles for College and University Teaching." *New Directions for Teaching and Learning* 66 (Summer 1996): 57–63.

Palmer, Parker J. "Good Talk about Good Teaching: Improving Teaching through Conversation and Community." Change 25:6 (November/December 1993) 8 –14.

Smith, Ronald A. "Reflecting on the Ethics and Values of Our Practice." *New Directions for Teaching and Learning* 66 (Summer 1996): 79–88.

NOTES

Jackman

1. Amy J. Phelps, "Teaching to Enhance Problem Solving," *Journal of Chemical Education* 73 (April 1996): 301; Mary B. Nakhleh, Kirsten A. Lowrey, & Richard C. Mitchell, "Narrowing the Gap between Concepts and Algorithms in Freshman Chemistry," *Journal of Chemical Education* 73 (August 1996): 758; Mary B. Nakhleh, "Are Our Students Conceptual Thinkers or Algorithmic Problem Solvers?" *Journal of Chemical Education* 70 (January 1993): 50; Mary B. Nakhleh and Richard C. Mitchell, "Concept Learning versus Problem Solving," *Journal of Chemical Education* 70 (March 1993): 190; Barbara A. Sawrey, "Concept Learning versus Problem Solving: Revised," *Journal of Chemical Education* 67 (March 1990): 253; Miles Pickering, "Further Studies on Concept Learning versus Problem Solving," *Journal of Chemical Education* 67 (March 1990): 254; Susan C. Nurrenberg and Miles Pickering, "Concept Learning versus Problem Solving: Is There a Difference?" *Journal of Chemical Education* 64 (June 1987): 508.

Kotilaine

1. On Drum Gahu, see David Locke, *Drum Gahu: The Rhythms of West African Drumming* (Crown Point, IN: White Cliffs Media, 1987).

2. This essay is meant to be only one "voice of experience" and thus will not attempt to provide a lengthy discourse on theories of race in the classroom. For this author, the most helpful by far of the numerous books and articles on this subject has been John A. Williams, *Classroom in Conflict: Teaching Controversial Subjects in a Diverse Society* (Albany: State University of New York, 1994).

Weiss

1. Bell, D. *The Coming of Post-industrial Society: A Venture in Social Forecasting.* (New York: Basic Books), 1973.

2. B. Wilson. "Dynamic Learning Communities: An Alternative to 'Designed Instructional Systems'." In *Proceedings of Selected Research and Development Presentations*

at the 1996 National Convention of the Association for Educational Communications and Technology (18th), Indianapolis, IN.: n.p., 1996, and M. Hamm. *The Collaborative Dimensions of Learning.* (Norwood, NJ: Ablex Publishing Corporation, 1992). For reviews of the literature on organizational learning, see: Argyris, Chris and Schon, Donald A. *Organizational Learning II: Theory, Method, and Practice.* (Reading, MA: Addison-Westley, 1996) pp. 180–99; G. Huber, "Organizational Learning: The Contributing Processes and the Literatures." *Organization Science 2* (1991): 88–115; B. Levitt and J. March. "Organizational Learning." *Annual Review of Sociology* 14 (1988): 319–40.

3. A.F. Osborn, *Applied Imagination.* 2nd ed. (New York: Scribner, 1957).

4. For an excellent discussion of brainstorming and its benefits in a corporate product development context, see R.I. Sutton and A. Hargadon, "Brainstorming Groups in Context: Effectiveness in a Product Design Firm." *Administrative Science Quarterly* 41 (1996): 685–718.

5. For a more detailed discussion of brainstorming and how to use this approach in discussion sessions, see A.F. Osborn, *Applied Imagination.* 2nd ed. (New York: Scribner, 1957).

6. D. McCormick and M. Kahn, "Barn Raising: Collaborative Group Process in Seminars," in L.B. Barnes, C.R. Christensen, and A.J. Hansen, eds. *Teaching and the Case Method.* 3rd ed (Boston: Harvard Business School Press, 1994), pp. 194–98.

7. For a more detailed discussion of barn raising and how to use this approach in discussion sessions, see D. McCormick and M. Kahn, "Barn Raising: Collaborative Group Process in Seminars," in L.B. Barnes, C.R. Christensen, and A.J. Hansen, eds., *Teaching and the Case Method.* 3rd ed. (Boston: Harvard Business School Press, 1994), pp. 194–98.

8. For additional information on how to use scenario planning, see P. Schoemaker, "Scenario Planning: A Tool for Strategic Thinking." *Sloan Management Review* (Winter, 1995): 25–40; P. Wack, "Scenarios: Shooting the Rapids." *Harvard Business Review* (November-December, 1985): 139–50.

9. L. Baloche. "Breaking Down the Walls: Integrating Creative Questioning and Cooperative Learning into the Social Studies." *Social Studies* 85 (1994): 25–30.

Dawes

1. For a review of related educational literature see C.C. Bonwell and J.A. Eison, *Active Learning: Creating Excitement in the Classroom,* ASHE-ERIC Higher Education Report no. 1. (Washington, D.C.: George Washington University, 1991); Joseph Lowman,

"Assignments that Promote and Integrate Learning," in *Teaching on Solid Ground: Using Scholarship to Improve Practice* (San Francisco: Jossey-Bass Publishers, 1996), pp. 205–31; Wilbert J. McKeachie, *Teaching Tips: Strategies, Research and Theory for College and University Teachers* (Lexington, MA: D.C. Heath, 1994), chapters 10, 31, 32; Wilbert J. McKeachie, *Teaching Tips: A Guidebook for the Beginning College Teacher* (Lexington, MA: D.C. Heath, 1986), chapters 23–25; Maryellen Weimer, *Improving Your Classroom Teaching: Survival Skills for Scholars*, vol. 1. (Newbury Park, CA: SAGE Publications, 1993), particularly chapters 1, 2, 4.

Winkelmes

1. A selected bibliography of recent literature on discussion in the classroom is provided at the end of this book. Chapters by Leigh Weiss, Eric Towne, Jennifer Kotilaine, and Jim Dawes published here address techniques that can enhance classroom discussions.

Rao

1. For a brief overview of some theories of student motivation, see Ann F. Lucas, "Using Psychological Models to Understand Student Motivation," *New Directions for Teaching and Learning* 42 (Summer 1990): 103–14. For more on active learning strategies see C.C. Bonwell and J.A. Eison, *Active Learning: Creating Excitement in the Classroom*, ASHE-ERIC Higher Education Report No. 1 (Washington, D.C.: George Washington University, 1991) and the other chapters in this volume.

2. Richard Light, "Explorations with Students and Faculty about Teaching, Learning, and Student Life: Second Report" *Report of the Harvard Assessment Seminars*, 1992, pp. 25–33.

3. This research is influenced by the work of the Russian psychologist Lev Vygotsky.

4. William G. Perry, *Forms of Intellectual and Ethical Development in the College Years: A Scheme*. (New York: Holt, Rinehart, and Winston, 1970).

5. Some claim that extrinsic motivation ultimately detracts from intrinsic motivation. For example see Joseph Lowman, "Promoting Motivation and Learning," *College Teaching* 38:4 (Fall 1990): 137.

6. For this and some of the following techniques I am indebted to the Graduate Writing Fellow Program organized by Sue Lonoff of the Derek Bok Center for Teaching and Learning at Harvard University.

7. Moreover, Barbara Bushey argues that students respond best when given concrete strategies for revision. See Barbara Bushey, "Writing Improvement in the Harvard

Expository Writing Program: Policy Recommendations, Suggestions for Faculty, and Suggestions for Students," *Report presented to President Derek Bok on behalf of the Harvard Assessment Seminars*, 1991.

8. The students I refer to in this essay are composites of the students I have taught at Harvard University.

9. Richard Light, "Explorations with Students and Faculty about Teaching, Learning, and Student Life: First Report" *Report of the Harvard Assessment Seminars*, 1990, pp. 31–33.

10. Ibid., pp. 31–33

11. Ibid., pp. 31–33.

Walk

1. One key method for improving student writing is to give students essay assignments that spell out in detail the thinking and writing tasks involved in producing a good essay—tasks such as analyzing a single text, comparing two or more texts, viewing one text through the "lens" of another, illuminating a central concept, and so on. You can also get better drafts by sequencing your writing assignments, that is, leading up to them with one or more pre-draft assignments: for example, finding and analyzing "hot spots" in a text, asking analytical questions, or writing a one-page paper proposal. See Gordon Harvey, "Asking for It: Imagining the Role of Student Writing." *ADE Bulletin* 116 (Spring 1997): 3–7.

2. Since the explosion of interest in collaborative learning in the early 1970s, writing groups have become a staple of many college composition and secondary school courses, as Anne Ruggles Gere has observed *in Writing Groups: History, Theory, and Implications* (Carbondale and Edwardsville: Southern Illinois University Press, 1987). I like the term "writing group," because professional writers use it to describe the groups they belong to, but, as Gere notes, writing groups go by many different names: "the partner method, helping circles, collaborative writing, response groups, team writing, writing laboratories, teacherless writing classes, group inquiry technique, the round table, class criticism, editing sessions, writing teams, workshops, peer tutoring, the socialized method, mutual improvement sessions, intensive peer review"(p. 1).

3. Nancy Sommers, *A Study of Undergraduate Writing at Harvard* (Cambridge: Expository Writing Program, Harvard University, 1994), pp. 14–15.

4. Gere, p. 125. Like other "collaborative learning situations," writing groups may also help "integrate nontraditional and ethnically or racially diverse students into the class," according to Rebecca Bell-Metereau ("Breaking Boundaries, Solving Problems, Giving Gifts: Student Empowerment in Small Group Work," *in Writing With: New Directions*

in Collaborative Teaching, ed. Sally Barr Reagan, Thomas Fox, and David Bleich [Albany: State University of New York Press, 1994], p. 249).

5. Nancy Sommers, "Revision Strategies of Student Writers and Experienced Adult Writers," *The Writing Teacher's Sourcebook*, 2nd ed., ed. Gary Tate and Edward P. J. Corbett (New York: Oxford University Press, 1988), pp. 122, 125.

6. For an excellent discussion of draft workshops, see Maxine Rodburg, "Workshops in the Teaching of Writing," in *How Writers Teach Writing*, ed. Nancy Kline (Englewood Cliffs, NJ: Prentice-Hall, Inc., 1992), pp. 143–56.

7. Ibid.

8. I would like to thank those friends and colleagues who helped me plan and revise this essay: Elizabeth Abrams, Noël Bisson, Alan Cooper, Philippa Hayward, Rhonda Rockwell, Dawn Skorczewski, Lee Warren, and Mary-Ann Winkelmes. My mother had a few things to say, too; her name is Nancy A. Walk.

Richardson

1. Craig Lambert, "Desperately Seeking Summa," *Harvard Magazine*, May-June 1993, p. 36.

2. Ibid., 40.

3. Parimal Patil, a resident tutor at Harvard's Currier House, as quoted in Lambert, 37.

4. See Margaret Placier, "'But I Have to Have an A': Probing the Cultural Meanings and Ethical Dilemmas of Grades in Teacher Education," paper presented at the Annual Meeting of the American Educational Research Association, Atlanta, Georgia, 12–16 April 1993, p. 3.

5. See James G. Nimmer, "Effects of Grading Practices and Time of Rating on Student Ratings of Faculty Performance and Student Learning," *Research in Higher Education* 32 (April 1991), which reports that "student ratings of college faculty were directly affected by grading practices."(They were also affected by when the evaluations were conducted). Anecdotal evidence also appears in Placier, p. 8: "Over time through practice and collaboration with colleagues, I have become...more selective about assigning A's. At the same time my teaching evaluations have gone from very positive to mediocre.... I have also had more conflicts with students about grades. At times I am tempted to revert to my initial leniency."

6. Eleanor Agnew, "Departmental Grade Quotas: The Silent Saboteur," paper presented at the 44th Annual Meeting of the Conference on College Composition and Communication, San Diego, California, 31 March–3 April 1993, p. 4.

7. Christopher M. Jedrey, "Grading and Evaluation," in Margaret Morganroth Gullette, ed., *The Art and Craft of Teaching* (Cambridge, Massachusetts: Harvard-Danforth Center for Teaching and Learning, 1984), p. 103.

8. Individual university or college teaching handbooks can provide helpful models of grading criteria.

9. Jedrey writes, "It is a matter of professional courtesy to take the work of every student seriously, even when it seems clear that the student does not…. It is best to err on the conservative side in these matters." Jedrey, p. 11.

10. See, for instance, Tracie Church Guzzio, "Collaborative Conclusions: Involving Students in the Evaluation Process," paper presented at the 47th Annual Meeting of the conference on College Composition and Communications, Milwaukee, Wisconsin, 27–30 March 1996, "Involving Students in Evaluation," *English Journal* 78 (November 1989): 75–77, and Laura Larson, "Making Writing Real: 'Rewrite Days' and Other Empowerments," *College Teaching* 43 (Fall 1995): 132–33, and Kerry Walk in this volume.

Bodner

1. John D. Bransford, and Marcia K. Johnson, "Considerations of some problems of comprehension," in *Visual Information Processing*, ed. William G. Chase (New York: Academic Press, 1973).

Fernald

1. A brief bibliography of recent literature on student-teacher conferences appears at the end of this chapter.

2. Richard L. Baker, Jr., "The Ethics of Student-Faculty Friendships," *New Directions for Teaching and Learning* 66 (Summer 1996): 26.

3. Kathryn Evans, "'That's Not What I Meant': Failures of Interpretation in the Writing Conference" (Bethesda, MD: ERIC Document Reproduction Service ED 375 399, 1994), p. 5.

4. Ibid.

5. Baker 1996, p. 30.

6. Ibid., p. 32.

BIBLIOGRAPHY

The topics that define this bibliography correspond to the central themes of the Senior Teaching Fellows' discussions. Each section of the bibliography has been revised according to the group's suggestions. The publications included here not only informed the fellows' discussions but also inspired them to contribute to the literature on teaching and learning with a collaborative publication of their own.

Mary-Ann Winkelmes

Overviews of Literature and Research on College and University Teaching

Feldman, Kenneth A. and Michael B. Paulsen, eds. *Teaching and Learning in the College Classroom*. Needham Heights, MA: Ginn Press, 1994.

McKeachie, Wilbert J. "Research on College Teaching: The Historical Background." *Journal of Educational Psychology* 82, no. 2 (1990): 189–200.

McKeachie, Wilbert J. et al. *Teaching and Learning in the College Classroom: A Review of the Research Literature*. Ann Arbor: University of Michigan, 1987.

Svinicki, Marilla D., Anastasia Hagen, and Debra K. Meyer. "How Research on Learning Strengthens Instruction." In *Teaching on Solid Ground: Using Scholarship to Improve Practice*. Edited by Robert J. Menges, Maryellen Weimer, et al. San Francisco: Jossey-Bass, 1996.

Weimer, Maryellen. "The Disciplinary Journals on Pedagogy." *Change* 25, no. 6 (November-December 1993): 44–51.

Effective Techniques Recommended by Successful Teachers

Beidler, Peter G., ed. *Distinguished Teachers on Effective Teaching*. New Directions for Teaching and Learning, no. 28. San Francisco: Jossey-Bass, 1986, chapters 5, 7.

Boice, Robert. "Quick Starters: New Faculty Who Succeed." In Theall, Michael and Jennifer Franklin, eds. *Effective Practices for Improving Teaching*. New Directions for Teaching and Learning, no. 48. San Francisco: Jossey-Bass, 1991, pp. 111–123.

Davis, Barbara Gross. *Tools for Teaching*. San Francisco: Jossey-Bass, 1993.

Eble, Kenneth E. *The Craft of Teaching: A Guide to Mastering the Professor's Art*. 2d ed. San Francisco: Jossey-Bass, 1988.

Ericksen, S.F. *The Essence of Good Teaching*. San Francisco: Jossey-Bass, 1984.

Feldman, Kenneth A. "Effective College Teaching from the Students' and Faculty's View: Matched or Mismatched Priorities." *Research in Higher Education* 28, no. 4 (June 1988): 291–344.

Feldman, Kenneth A., ed. *Teaching and Learning in the College Classroom*. ASHE Reader Series. Needham Heights, MA: Ginn Press, 1994.

Gamson, Zelda F. "A Brief History of the Seven Principles for Good Practice in Undergraduate Education." *Applying the Seven Principles for Good Practice in Undergraduate Education*. New Directions for Teaching & Learning, no. 47. San Francisco: Jossey-Bass, 1991, pp. 5–12.

Henry, Martha A. "Differentiating the Expert and Experienced Teacher: Quantitative Differences in Instructional Decision Making." Paper presented at Annual Meeting of American Association of Colleges for Teacher Education (Chicago, Feb. 16–19, 1994).

Lee, Virginia S. "The Uses of Uncertainty in the College Classroom." *Teaching Excellence: Toward the Best in the Academy (A Publication of the Professional and Organizational Development Network in Higher Education)* 10, no. 4 (1998–1999).

Lowman, J. *Mastering the Techniques of Teaching*. San Francisco: Jossey-Bass, 1984.

Marcroft, Minette. "The Politics of the Classroom: Toward an Oppositional Pedagogy." In *Excellent Teaching in a Changing Academy: Essays in Honor of Kenneth Eble*. Edited by Feroza Jussawalla. New Directions for Teaching and Learning, no. 44. San Francisco: Jossey-Bass, 1990, pp. 61–71.

McKeachie, Wilbert J. *Teaching Tips: Strategies, Research and Theory for College and University Teachers*. Lexington, MA: D.C. Heath, 1994.

Murray, Harry G. "Classroom Teaching Behaviors Related to College Teaching Effectiveness." In *Using Research to Improve Teaching*. Edited by Janet Donald and Arthur Sullivan. New Directions for Teaching and Learning, no. 23. San Francisco: Jossey-Bass, 1985, pp. 21–34.

Palmer, Parker J. "Good Talk about Good Teaching: Improving Teaching through Conversation and Community." *Change* (November-December 1993): 8–13.

Palmer, Parker J. "Good Teaching: A Matter of Living the Mystery." In *Teaching and the Case Method*. 3d ed. Edited by Louis B. Barnes, C. Roland Christensen and Abby J. Hansen. Boston: Harvard Business School Press, 1994, pp. 327–32.

Velenchik, Ann D. "The Case Method as a Strategy for Teaching Policy Analysis to Undergraduates." *The Journal of Economic Education* 1 (Winter 1995): 29–38.

Walsh, Anthony J. "A Coaching Model for the Teaching of Writing." In *Excellent Teaching in a Changing Academy: Essays in Honor of Kenneth Eble*. Edited by Feroza Jussawalla. New Directions for Teaching and Learning, no. 44. San Francisco: Jossey-Bass, 1990, pp. 53–59.

Warren, Thomas, ed. *A View from the Academy: Liberal Arts Professors on Excellent Teaching*. New York and London: University Press of America, 1992.

Weimer, Maryellen. *Improving Your Classroom Teaching*. Survival Skills for Scholars 1. Newbury Park, CA: SAGE Publications, 1993. Particularly chapters 1, 2, 4.

Weimer, Maryellen. *Improving College Teaching*. San Francisco: Jossey-Bass, 1990.

Weimer, Maryellen. "Why Scholarship Is the Bedrock of Good Teaching." In *Teaching on Solid Ground: Using Scholarship to Improve Practice*. Edited by Robert J. Menges, Maryellen Weimer, et al. San Francisco: Jossey-Bass, 1996.

Wilkinson, James and John Boehrer. "Crossing the Rubicon: Twenty-four Faculty Transform Their Teaching." *Change* (November-December 1993): 52–58.

Teacher Motivation/Student Motivation

Bean, John C. *Engaging Ideas: The Professor's Guide to Integrating Writing, Critical Thinking, and Active Learning in the Classroom*. San Francisco: Jossey-Bass, 1996.

Beidler, Peter G., ed. *Distinguished Teachers on Effective Teaching*. New Directions for Teaching and Learning, no. 28. San Francisco: Jossey-Bass, 1986, chapter 6.

Bess, James L. *Teaching Well and Liking It: Motivating Professors to Teach Effectively* Baltimore: Johns Hopkins University Press, 1996.

Bonwell, C.C. and Eison, J.A. *Active Learning: Creating Excitement in the Classroom*. ASHE-ERIC Higher Education Report, no. 1. Washington, D.C.: George Washington University, 1991.

Coles, Robert. *The Call of Stories: Teaching and the Moral Imagination*. Boston, MA: Houghton Mifflin Co., 1989.

Covey, Stephen R. *Principle-Centered Leadership*. New York: Summit Books, 1991.

———. *The Seven Habits of Highly Effective People*. New York: Simon and Schuster, 1989.

Ericksen, S.F. *The Essence of Good Teaching*. San Francisco: Jossey-Bass, 1984, chap. 12 "Sustaining Good Teaching Over Time."

Fleisher, Carol L. *The Truth about Teachers (videorecording)*. Produced by Arnold Shapiro in association with USAA. Santa Monica, CA: Pyramid Film & Video, 1989.

Gardner, Howard. *Extraordinary Minds: Portraits of Exceptional Individuals and an Examination of Our Extraordinariness*. New York: Basic Books, 1997.

Hutchings, Pat. *Using Cases to Improve College Teaching*. Washington, D.C.: American Association for Higher Education, 1993.

Keeley, Stuart M. et al. "Coping with Student Resistance to Critical Thinking." *College Teaching* 43, no. 4 (Fall 1995): 140–45.

Light, Richard J. *Explorations with Students and Faculty about Teaching, Learning, and Student Life*. The Harvard Assessment Seminars, 1st report. Cambridge, MA: Harvard University Graduate School of Education and Kennedy School of Government, 1990.

——— *Explorations with Students and Faculty about Teaching, Learning, and Student Life*. The Harvard Assessment Seminars, 2d report. Cambridge, MA: Harvard University Graduate School of Education and Kennedy School of Government, 1992.

Lipson, Abigail and David Perkins. *Block—Getting Out of Your Own Way: The New Psychology of Counterintentional Behavior in Everyday Life*. New York: Carol Pub. Group, 1990.

Lonoff, Sue. "Using Videotape to Talk about Teaching." *ADE Bulletin* 118 (Winter 1997): 10–14.

Lowman, Joseph. "Assignments that Promote and Integrate Learning." In *Teaching on Solid Ground: Using Scholarship to Improve Practice*. Edited by Robert J. Menges, Maryellen Weimer, et al. San Francisco: Jossey-Bass, 1996, pp. 205–31.

Machell, David F. "A Professor Realizes the Potential Poison of Ivy." *Innovative Higher Education* 16, no. 2 (Winter 1991): 173–85.

McKeachie, Wilbert J. *Teaching Tips: Strategies, Research and Theory for College and University Teachers*. Lexington, MA: D.C. Heath, 1994, chapters 10, 31, 32.

———. *Teaching Tips: A Guidebook for the Beginning College Teacher*. Lexington, MA: D.C. Heath, 1986, chapters 23–25.

Perry, Raymond P., Verena H. Menec, and C. Ward Struthers. "Student Motivation from the Teacher's Perspective." In *Teaching on Solid Ground: Using Scholarship to Improve Practice*. Edited by Robert J. Menges, Maryellen Weimer, et al. San Francisco: Jossey-Bass, 1996.

Perry, William Graves. *Forms of Intellectual and Ethical Development in the College Years: A Scheme*. New York: Holt, Rinehart and Winston, 1970.

Pintrich, Paul." The Dynamic Interplay of Student Motivation and Cognition in the College Classroom." In *Advances in Motivations and Achievement: Motivation Enhancing Environments*, vol. 6. Edited by M. Maehr and C. Ames. New York: JAI Press, 1989. Reprinted in Kenneth A. Feldman and Michael B. Paulsen, eds. *Teaching and Learning in the College Classroom*. Needham Heights, MA: Ginn Press, 1994.

Pintrich, Paul R., D.R. Brown, and C.E. Weinstein. *Student Motivation, Cognition, and Learning: Essays in Honor of Wilbert J. McKeachie*. Hillsdale, NJ: Lawrence Erlbaum, 1994.

Rosenthal, Robert. "How Students Learn: Part II." *On Teaching and Learning: The Journal of the Harvard Danforth Center for Teaching and Learning* (April 1989): 22–27.

———. and Lenore Jacobson. *Pygmalion in the Classroom: Teacher Expectation and Pupils' Intellectual Development*. Robert Rosenthal, Lenore Jacobson. New York, NY: Irvington, 1992.

Scheurman, Geoffrey, "Professors' Beliefs and Assumptions Regarding Reasoning Abilities of
      College Students." In *Thinking about Thinking: A Constructivist Approach to Critical
      Thinking in the College Curriculum*. Edited by Thomas J. Russo. Educational Resources
      Information Center: ERIC Document Reproduction Service (EDRS), 1995, chapter 2.
Seldin, Peter, ed. Coping with Faculty Stress. New Directions for Teaching and Learning,
      no. 29. San Francisco: Jossey-Bass, 1987.

Seymour, Elaine and Nancy M. Hewitt. *Talking about Leaving: Why Undergraduates Leave
      the Sciences*. Boulder, CO: Westview Press, 1997.

Tobias, Sheila. *They're Not Dumb, They're Different: Stalking the Second Tier*. Tucson, AZ:
      Research Corp., 1990.

Velenchik, Ann D. "The Case Method as a Strategy for Teaching Policy Analysis to
      Undergraduates." *The Journal of Economic Education* 1 (winter 1995): 29–38.

Walker, Charles J. and Jennifer Woods Quinn. "Fostering Instructional Vitality and
      Motivation." In *Teaching on Solid Ground: Using Scholarship to Improve Practice*. Edited
      by Robert J. Menges, Maryellen Weimer, et al. San Francisco: Jossey-Bass, 1996.

Walvoord, Barbara E. and Virginia Johnson Anderson. *Effective Grading: A Tool for Learning
      and Assessment*. San Francisco: Jossey-Bass, 1998.

Weimer, Maryellen. *Improving Your Classroom Teaching*. Survival Skills for Scholars, no. 1.
      Newbury Park, CA: SAGE Publications, 1993, chapter 2.

Whitman, Neal A., David C. Spendlove, and Claire H. Clark. *Increasing Students' Learning:
      A Faculty Guide to Reducing Stress among Students*. ASHE-ERIC Higher Education
      Report, no. 4. Washington D.C.: ERIC Clearinghouse on Higher Education;
      Association for the Study of Higher Education, 1986.

Wlodkowski, Raymond J. Enhancing Adult Motivation to Learn: A Comprehensive Guide
      for Teaching All Adults. San Francisco: Jossey-Bass, 1999.

Discussion in the Classroom

Brookfield, Stephen D. "Preparing for Discussion." In *The Skillful Teacher: On Technique, Trust, and Responsiveness in the Classroom*. San Francisco and Oxford: Jossey-Bass, 1990, chapter 7, pp. 88–101 (chapter 9 on role-playing).

Carbone, Elisa. "Listening in the Classroom: A Two-way Street." *Teaching Excellence: Toward the Best in the Academy (A Publication of the Professional and Organizational Development Network in Higher Education)* 10, no. 4 (1998–1999).

Carlson, John A. and David W. Schodt,. "Beyond the Lecture: Case Teaching and the Learning of Economic Theory." *Economic Education* 26, 1 (Winter 1995): 17–28.

Christensen, C. Roland. "Premises and Practices of Discussion Teaching." In *Teaching and the Case Method*. Edited by Louis B. Barnes, C. Roland Christensen and Abby J. Hansen. Boston: Harvard Business School Press, 1994, pp. 23–33.

Christensen, C. Roland, David A. Garvin, and Ann Sweet, eds. *Education for Judgment: The Artistry of Discussion Leadership*. Boston: Harvard Business School Press, 1991.

Frederick, Peter. "The Dreaded Discussion: Ten Ways to Start." In *Teaching and the Case Method*, 1994, pp. 23–33.

Garcia, Reloy. "Twelve Ways of Looking at a Blackboard." *The Teaching Professor* 8, no. 5 (1991): 5–6.

Gullette, Margaret M. "Leading Discussion in a Lecture Course: Some Maxims and an Exhortation." *Change* 24, no. 2 (March-April 1992): 32–39.

Hughes Caplow, Julie A. and CarolAnne M. Kardash. "Collaborative Learning Activities in Graduate Courses." *Innovative Higher Education* 19, no. 3 (Spring 1995): 207–221.

Hutchings, Pat. *Using Cases to Improve College Teaching*. Washington, D.C.: American Association for Higher Education, 1993.

Matthews, Roberta S. "Collaborative Learning: Creating Knowledge with Students." In *Teaching on Solid Ground: Using Scholarship to Improve Practice*. Edited by Robert J. Menges, Maryellen Weimer, et al. San Francisco: Jossey-Bass, 1996.

McCormich, Don and Michael Kahn. "Barn Raising: Collaborative Group Process in Seminars." In *Teaching and the Case Method*, 1994, pp. 194–98.

McKeachie, Wilbert. *Teaching Tips: Strategies, Research and Theory for College and University Teachers*. Lexington, MA: D.C. Heath, 1994, chapter 4 "Organizing Effective

Discussions," and 1999 edition, chapter 5 "Facilitating Discussion: Posing Problems, Listening, Questioning."

Neff, Rose Ann and Maryellen Weimer. *Classroom Communication: Collected Readings for Effective Discussion and Questioning*. Madison, WI: Magna, 1989.

Rogers, Carl R. and Richard E. Farson. "Active Listening." In *Teaching and the Case Method*. 2d ed. Edited by C. Roland Christensen and Abby J. Hansen. Boston: Harvard Business School Press, 1987, pp. 166–74.

Sarkisian, Ellen. "Case Discussions on Teaching in the School of Public Health." *Change* (Nov-Dec 1993): 42–43.

Tannen, Deborah. *Gender and Discourse*. New York: Oxford University Press, 1994.

Tiberius, Richard G. *Small Group Teaching: A Trouble-shooting Guide*. Monograph Series, no. 22. Toronto, Ontario: Ontario Institute for Studies in Education Press, 1990.

Velenchik, Ann. "The Case Method as a Strategy for Teaching Undergraduates." *Journal of Economic Education* 26, no. 1 (Winter 1995): 29–38.

Weimer, Maryellen. "Stimulating Student Thought and Interest." In *Improving Your Classroom Teaching*. Survival Skills for Scholars, no. 1. Newbury Park, CA: SAGE Publications, 1993, chapter 4.

Welty, William M. "Discussion Method Teaching: How to Make It Work." *Change* (July-Aug 1989): 41–49.

Williams, John A. "Rules of Discussion." In *Classroom in Conflict: Teaching Controversial Subjects in a Diverse Society*. Albany: State University of New York, 1994, chapter 15.

Collaborative Learning

Much of the literature on collaborative learning focuses on two areas: 1) collaboration in writing instruction, 2) collaboration via computer, particularly for distance learning programs. Publications on collaborative learning groups consisting of teachers focus primarily on elementary and secondary school teachers and special education teachers.

This bibliography does not include publications in these three popular areas. Instead it includes a small selection of writings that will stimulate further thought about: 1) specific collaborative learning exercises we could adapt for use in our classrooms, 2) the ultimate purposes and goals we work towards when we use collaborative learning procedures.

Berry, Lemuel, Jr. *Collaborative Learning: A Program for Improving the Retention of Minority Students*. Educational Resources Information Center: ERIC Document Reproduction Service (EDRS), 1991.

Bocchi, Joseph. *Collaborative Learning in the Classroom Context: Toward an Integrated View of Communities*. Educational Resources Information Center: ERIC Document Reproduction Service (EDRS), 1989.

Bonwell, C.C. and Eison, J.A. *Active Learning: Creating Excitement in the Classroom*. ASHE-ERIC Higher Education Report, no. 1. Washington, D.C.: George Washington University, 1991

Bosworth, Kris and Sharon J. Hamilton, eds. *Collaborative Learning: Underlying Processes and Effective Techniques*. New Directions for Teaching and Learning, no. 59. San Francisco: Jossey-Bass, 1994.

Bouton, Clark and Russel Y. Garth, eds. *Learning in Groups*. New Directions For Teaching and Learning, no. 14. San Francisco: Jossey-Bass, 1983.

Bruffee, Kenneth A. *Collaborative Learning: Higher Education, Interdependence, and the Authority of Knowledge*. Baltimore: Johns Hopkins University Press, 1993.

Carroll, E. Ruth. "Improved Interpersonal Relationships: A Result of Group Learning." *Journal of Business and Technical Communication* 5, no. 3 (July1991): 285–99.

Derek Bok Center for Teaching and Learning. *Thinking Together: Collaborative Learning in Science* [videotape]. Cambridge: President and Fellows of Harvard University, 1992.

Flynn, Elizabeth A. et al. "Gender and Modes of Collaboration in a Chemical Engineering Design Course." *Journal of Business and Technical Communication* 5, no. 4 (Oct 1991): 444–62.

Foyle, Harvey C., ed. Interactive Learning in the Higher Education Classroom: Cooperative, Collaborative, and Active Learning Strategies. Washington, D.C.: National Education Association, 1995.

Garland, May. The Mathematics Workshop Model: An Interview with Uri Treisman. *Journal of Developmental Education* 16, no. 3 (Spring 1993): 14–22.

Goodsell, Anne S., M.R. Maher, and V. Tinto, eds. Collaborative Learning: *A Sourcebook for Higher Education*. University Park, PA: National Center on Postsecondary Teaching, Learning and Assessment, 1992.

Hamilton, Sharon J. and Edmund Hansen, eds. Collaborative Learning: Sourcebook for *Collaborative Learning in the Arts and Sciences at Indiana University*. Educational Resources Information Center: ERIC Document Reproduction Service (EDRS), 1992.

Kasturiarachi, A. Bathi. "Promoting Excellence in Undergraduate Mathematics through Workshops Based on Collaborative Learning." *Primus*, v. 7, n. 2 (June 1997): 147–63.

Light, Richard J. "The Harvard Assessment Seminars: Explorations with Students and Faculty about Teaching, Learning, and Student Life." First Report, 1990.

Matthews, Roberta S. et al. "Building Bridges Between Cooperative and Collaborative Learning." Change 27, no. 4 (July-Aug 1995): 34–37.

McCarthy, Lucille Parkinson. "Boundary Conversations: Conflicting Ways of Knowing in Philosophy and Interdisciplinary Research." *Research in the Teaching of English* 25, no. 4 (Dec 1991): 419–68.

MacGregor, Jean. "Collaborative Learning: Shared Inquiry as a Process of Reform." In *The Changing Face of College Teaching*. Edited by Marilla D. Svinicki. New Directions for Teaching and Learning, no. 42. San Francisco: Jossey-Bass, 1990, pp. 19–30.

McKeachie, Wilbert. *Teaching Tips: Strategies, Research and Theory for College and University Teachers*. Lexington, MA: D.C. Heath, 1994, chapter 13, "Peer Learning."

Meltzer, David E. "Promoting Interactivity in Physics Lecture Classes." *The Physics Teacher* 34, no. 2 (Feb 1996): 72ff.

National Institute for Science Education. "Collaborative Learning: Small Group Learning Page." http://www.wcer.wisc.edu/nise/CL1/CL/clhome.asp (Click on "resources.")

Rau, William. "Humanizing the College Classroom: Collaborative Learning and Social Organization among Students." *Teaching Sociology* 18, no. 2 (April 1990): 141–55.

Rosenthal, Robert. "How Students Learn: Part II." *On Teaching and Learning: The Journal of the Harvard Danforth Center* (April 1989): 22–27.

Sarkisian, Ellen. "Working in Groups: A Note to Faculty and a Quick Guide for Students." Cambridge: Derek Bok Center for Teaching and Learning, 1984.

Schomberg, Steven F. et al. *Strategies for Active Teaching and Learning in University Classrooms: A Handbook of Teaching Strategies*. Educational Resources Information Center: ERIC Document Reproduction Service (EDRS), 1988.

Smith, Karl A. "Cooperative Learning: Making 'Groupwork' Work." In *Using Active Learning in College Classes: A Range of Options for Faculty*. Edited by Tracey E. Sutherland and Charles C. Bonwell. New Directions for Teaching and Learning 67. San Francisco: Jossey-Bass, 1996.

Tiberius, Richard G. *Small Group Teaching: A Trouble-shooting Guide*. Monograph Series, no. 22. Toronto, Ontario: Ontario Institute for Studies in Education Press, 1990.

Treisman, Uri. "Studying Students Studying Calculus: A Look at the Lives of Minority Mathematics Students in College." *College Mathematics Journal* 23, no. 5 (November 1992): 362–72.

Trimbur, John. "Consensus and Difference in Collaborative Learning. *College English* 51, no. 6 (Oct 1989): 602–16.

Weimer, Maryellen. "Stimulating Student Thought and Interest." In *Improving Your Classroom Teaching*. Survival Skills for Scholars. no. 1. Newbury Park, CA: SAGE Publications, 1993, chapter 4.

Grading and Feedback on Students' Work

Agnew, Eleanor. "Departmental Grade Quotas: The Silent Saboteur." Paper presented at the 44th Annual Meeting of the Conference on College Composition and Communication, San Diego, California, 31 March-3 April 1993.

Angelo, Thomas A. "Classroom Assessment: Improving Learning Quality Where It Matters Most." In Marilla D. Svinicki, ed., *The Changing Face of College Teaching*. New Directions for Teaching and Learning 42. San Francisco: Jossey-Bass, 1990, chapter 6.

————— and K. Patricia Cross. *Classroom Assessment Techniques: A Handbook for College Teachers*. 2d ed.San Francisco: Jossey-Bass, 1993.

Braxton, John M. et al. "Anticipatory Socialization of Undergraduate College Teaching Norms by Entering Teaching Assistants." *Research in Higher Education* 36 (December 1995): 671–86.

Davis, Barbara Gross. "Demystifying Assessment: Learning from the Field of Evaluation." In Peter J. Gray, ed., *Achieving Assessment Goals Using Evaluation Techniques*. New Directions for Higher Education 67. San Francisco: Jossey-Bass, Inc., 1989, pp. 5–20 (an overview of the literature and state of research)

—————. "Grading Practices." In *Tools for Teaching*. San Francisco: Jossey-Bass, 1993, chapter 32.

Dey, Eric L., and others. "Does Being Student-Centered Lead to Academic Standards? Faculty Orientations and Grading Practices." Paper presented at the 35th Annual Forum of the Association for Institutional Research, Boston, Massachusetts, 28–31 May 1995.

Donald, Janet. "Using Assessment to Define Tasks and Measure Learning." In *Improving the Environment for Learning: Academic Leaders Talk About What Works*. San Francisco: Jossey Bass, 1997, pp. 161–191.

Erickson, Stanford C. "Assessing the Achievement of Each Student." In *The Essence of Good Teaching*. San Francisco: Jossey-Bass, 1988, chapter 9.

Guskey, Thomas R. "Making the Grade: What Benefits Students?" *Educational Leadership* 52 (October 1994): 14–20.

Guzzio, Tracie Church. "Collaborative Conclusions: Involving Students in the Evaluation Process." Paper presented at the 47th Annual Meeting of the Conference on College Composition and Communications, Milwaukee, Wisconsin, 27–30 March 1996.

"Involving Students in Evaluation." *English Journal* 78 (November 1989): 75–77.

Jedrey, Christopher M. "Grading and Evaluation." in *The Art and Craft of Teaching*, pp. 103–15. Edited by Margaret Morganroth Gullette. Cambridge, MA: Harvard-Danforth Center for Teaching and Learning, 1984.

Lambert, Craig. "Desperately Seeking Summa." *Harvard Magazine*, May-June 1993, pp. 36–40.

Larson, Laura. "Making Writing Real: 'Rewrite Days' and Other Empowerments." *College Teaching* 43 (Fall 1995): 132–33.

Light, Richard J. *Explorations with Students and Faculty about Teaching, Learning, and Student Life*. The Harvard Assessment Seminars, 1st report. Cambridge, MA: Harvard University Graduate School of Education and Kennedy School of Government, 1990.

Lowman, Joseph. "Evaluating Student Performance." In *Mastering the Techniques of Teaching*. 2d ed. San Francisco: Jossey-Bass, 1995, pp. 251–85.

McKeachie, Wilbert J. "Testing and Assessing Learning" and "The ABC's of Assigning Grades." *In Teaching Tips: Strategies, Research, and Theory for College and University Teachers*. 10th ed. Boston and New York: Houghton Mifflin, 1999, chapters 7 and 9.

Nimmer, James G. "Effects of Grading Practices and Time of Rating on Student Ratings of Faculty Performance and Student Learning." *Research in Higher Education* 32 (April 1991): 195–215.

Ohmer, Milton, Howard R. Pollio and James A. Eison. *Making Sense of College Grades : Why the Grading System Does Not Work and What Can Be Done about It*. San Francisco: Jossey-Bass Publishers, 1986.

Pintrich, Paul R. and Glenn Ross Johnson, "Assessing and Improving Students' Learning Strategies." In Marilla D. Svinicki, ed., *The Changing Face of College Teaching*. New Directions for Teaching and Learning 42. San Francisco: Jossey-Bass, 1990, chapter 7.

Placier, Margaret. "'But I Have to Have an A': Probing the Cultural Meanings and Ethical Dilemmas of Grades in Teacher Education." Paper presented at the Annual Meeting of the American Educational Research Association, Atlanta, Georgia, 12–16 April 1993.

Pollio, Howard R. and W. Lee Humphreys. "Grading Students." In Maryellen Weimer and Rose Ann Neff, eds., *Teaching College: Collected Readings for the New Instructor*. Madison, WI: Atwood Publishing, 1998.

Walvoord, Barbara E. and Virginia Johnson Anderson. *Effective Grading: A Tool for Learning and Assessment*. San Francisco: Jossey-Bass, 1998.

Weimer, Maryellen. "Assessing Their Learning and Your Teaching." *In Improving Your Classroom Teaching*. Survival Skills for Scholars 1. London: SAGE Publications, 1996, chapter 7.

Diversity and Communication

Ansell, Helen and James Wilkinson, eds. *On Teaching and Learning: Journal of the Derek Bok Center, Harvard University* 4 (1992) [special issue on gender and learning].

Bowen, William G. and Derek C. Bok. *The Shape of the River: Long-term Consequences of Considering Race in College and University Admissions.* Princeton, NJ: Princeton University Press, 1998.

Cain, William E., ed. *Teaching the Conflicts: Gerald Graff, Curricular Reform, and the Culture Wars.* New York: Garland, 1994.

Gardner, Howard. *Frames of Mind: The Theory of Multiple Intelligences.* New York: Basic Books, 1983.

Gmelch, Sharon Bohn. *Gender on Campus: Issues for College Women.* New Brunswick, NJ: Rutgers University Press, 1998.

Handbook on Race Relations and the Common Pursuit. Cambridge, MA: Office of the Dean of Students and President and Fellows of Harvard College, 1996.

Hummel, Mary and Claude Steele. "The Learning Community: A Program to Address Issues of Academic Achievement and Retention." *Journal of Intergroup Relations* 23 no. 2 (Summer 1996): 28–32.

Kors, Alan C. and Harvey A. Silverglate *The Shadow University: The Betrayal of Liberty on America's Campuses.* New York : Free Press, 1998.

McIntosh, Peggy. "White Privilege and Male Privilege." Working Paper Series, Wellesley College Center for Research on Women, Publications Department, no. 189, 1988.

McKeachie, Wilbert. *Teaching Tips: Strategies, Research and Theory for College and University Teachers.* Lexington, MA: D.C. Heath, 1994, chapter 24: "Problem Situations."

Perry, W.G. *Forms of Intellectual and Ethical Development in the College Years: A Scheme.* New York: Holt, Rinehart and Winston, 1970.

Race in the Classroom: The Multiplicity of Experience (videotape). Cambridge, MA: Derek Bok Center for Teaching and Learning, and President and Fellows of Harvard College, 1992 and *Facilitator's Guide for Race in the Classroom.* Cambridge, MA: Derek Bok Center for Teaching and Learning, Office of Race Relations and Minority Affairs, and President and Fellows of Harvard College, 1992 [Distributed by Anker Publishing, Bolton, MA].

Sarkisian, Ellen. *Teaching American Students: A Guide for International Faculty and Teaching Assistants in Colleges and Universities.* Revised ed. Cambridge, MA: President and Fellows of Harvard University, Derek Bok Center for Teaching and Learning, 1997.

Schmeck, Ronald R., ed. *Learning Strategies and Learning Styles.* New York, NY: Plenum, 1988.

Schwartz, Peter and Webb, Graham. *Case Studies on Teaching in Higher Education.* London: Kogan Page Ltd., 1993.

Steele, Claude M. "Race and the Schooling of Black Americans." *Atlantic* 269, no. 4 (April 1992): 68–78.

Svinicki, Marilla. "Creating a Foundation for Instructional Decisions." In *The Professional Development of Graduate Teaching Assistants.* Edited by Michele Marincovich. Bolton, MA: Anker, 1998.

Tannen, Deborah. *Gender and Discourse.* New York: Oxford University Press, 1994.

Tatum, Beverly Daniel. "Talking about Race, Learning about Racism: The Application of Racial Identity Development Theory in the Classroom." *Harvard Educational Review* 62, no. 1 (Spring, 1992).

———. *"Why Are All the Black Kids Sitting Together in the Cafeteria?" and Other Conversations about the Development of Racial Identity.* New York: Basic Books, 1997.

Teaching Fellows Handbook, 1998–1999. Cambridge, MA: Graduate School of Arts and Sciences and President and Fellows of Harvard University. (See bibliographies on discussion leading, gender issues, race issues.)

Thernstrom, Abigail M. *School Choice in Massachusetts.* Boston, MA: Pioneer Institute for Public Policy Research, 1991.

Tiberius, Richard G. *Small Group Teaching: A Trouble-shooting Guide.* Monograph Series, no. 22. Toronto, Ontario: Ontario Institute for Studies in Education Press, 1990.

"Tips for Teachers: Encouraging Students in a Racially Diverse Classroom." Cambridge, MA: Derek Bok Center for Teaching and Learning, and Office for Race Relations and Minority Affairs, 1992. [http://www.fas.harvard.edu/~bok_cen]

"Tips for Teachers: Sensitivity to Women in the Contemporary Classroom." Cambridge, MA: Derek Bok Center for Teaching and Learning, and President and Fellows of Harvard University, 1994. [http://www.fas.harvard.edu/~bok_cen]

Tobias, Sheila. *They're Not Dumb, They're Different: Stalking the Second Tier.* Tucson, AZ: Research Corp., 1990.

Treisman, Uri. "Studying Students Studying Calculus: A Look at the Lives of Minority Mathematics Students in College." *College Mathematics Journal* 23, no. 5 (November 1992): 362–72.

Warren, Lee. "Class in the Classroom." *Teaching Excellence: Toward the Best in the Academy (A Publication of the Professional and Organizational Development Network in Higher Education)* 10, no. 2 (1998–1999).

Williams, John A. Classroom in Conflict: *Teaching Controversial Subjects in a Diverse Society.* Albany, NY: State University of New York Press, 1994.

Women in the Classroom: Cases for Discussion (videotape). Cambridge, MA: Derek Bok Center for Teaching and Learning, and President and Fellows of Harvard College, 1996 and *Facilitator's Guide for Women in the Classroom.* Cambridge, MA: Derek Bok Center for Teaching and Learning, and President and Fellows of Harvard College, 1996 [Distributed by Anker Publishing, Bolton, MA].

Balancing Teaching and Professional Concerns

Baldwin, R. G. "Faculty Career Stages and Implications for Professional Development." In J. H. Schuster, D. W. Wheeler, and Associates, eds. Enhancing Faculty Careers: Strategies for Development and Renewal. San Francisco: Jossey-Bass, 1990, pp. 20–30.

Boice, Robert. "Developing Writing, Then Teaching, Amongst New Faculty." *Research in Higher Education* 36, no. 4 (1995): 415–56.

———. "Quick Starters: New Faculty Who Succeed." In *Effective Practices for Improving Teaching*. Edited by Michael Theall and Jennifer Franklin. New Directions for Teaching and Learning, no. 48. San Francisco: Jossey-Bass, 1991, pp. 111–23.

Davis, Barbara Gross. *Tools for Teaching*. San Francisco: Jossey-Bass, 1993.

DeNeef, A. Leigh, ed. *The Academic's Handbook*, 2d ed. Durham, NC: Duke University Press, 1995.

Edgerton, Russell, Patricia Hutchins, and Kathleen Quinlan. *The Teaching Portfolio: Capturing the Scholarship in Teaching*. Washington, D.C.: American Association for Higher Education, 1991.

Farber, Barry A. *Crisis in Education: Stress and Burnout in the American Teacher*. San Francisco and Oxford: Jossey-Bass, 1991, particularly chapters 1, 2, 10.

Gmelch, Walter. "Balance Your Personal and Professional Pressures." In *Coping with Faculty Stress*. Survival Skills for Scholars 5. Thousand Oaks, CA: SAGE, 1993.

Gold, Yvonne. "Reducing Stress and Burnout through Induction Programs." *Action in Teacher Education* 11, no. 3 (fall 1989): 66–70.

Heath, Douglas. *Faculty Burnout, Morale and Vocational Adaptation*. Boston: National Association of Independent Schools, 1981.

Jarvis, Donald K. *Junior Faculty Development: A Handbook*. New York: Modern Language Association, 1991.

Kieffer, Jonathan C. "Using a Problem-Focused Coping Strategy on Teacher Stress and Burnout." *Teaching and Change* 1, no. 2 (Winter 1994): 190–206.

McGuire, Willard H. "Teacher Stress and Burnout." In *Education in the 80s: Curricular Challenges*. Edited by Lois V. Edinger et al. Washington, D.C.: NEA, 1981.

McKeachie, Wilbert J. *Teaching Tips: Strategies, Research, and Theory for College and University Teachers*. 10th ed. Boston and New York: Houghton Mifflin, 1999, (especially chapter 2).

Melendez, Winifred A. and Rafael M. de Guzman. *Burnout: The New Academic Disease*. ASHE-ERIC/Higher Education Research Report, no. 9. Washington, D.C.: Association for the Study of Higher Education, 1983.

Parsons, Paul. *Getting Published: The Acquisition Process at University Presses*. Knoxville: University of Tennessee Press, 1989.

Reisman, David; Bell, Daniel; Vendler, Helen; Gould, Stephen Jay. "Balancing Teaching and Writing." *On Teaching and Learning* (January 1987): 11–16.

Schor, Juliet. *The Overworked American: The Unexpected Decline of Leisure*. New York, NY: Basic Books, 1992

Seldin, Peter. *The Teaching Portfolio: A Practical Guide to Improved Performance and Promotion/Tenure Decisions*. Bolton, MA: Anker, 1991.

Seldin, Peter, ed., *Coping with Faculty Stress*. New Directions for Teaching and Learning, no. 29. San Francisco: Jossey-Bass, 1987.

Smedley, Christine S. *Getting Your Book Published*. Survival Skills for Scholars 10. Thousand Oaks, CA: SAGE, 1993. Particularly chapters 2, 4, 5.

Sorcinelli, Mary Deane. "New and Junior Faculty Stress: Research and Responses." In *Developing New and Junior Faculty*. Edited by Mary Deane Sorcinelli and Ann E. Austin. New Directions for Teaching and Learning, no. 50. San Francisco: Jossey-Bass, 1992, pp. 27–37.

Sparks, Dennis and Hammond, Janice. *Managing Teacher Stress and Burnout*. ERIC Clearinghouse, 1981.

Tannen, Deborah. "The Power of Talk: Who Gets Heard and Why." *Harvard Business Review* (Sept-Oct 1995): 138–50.

Thyer, Bruce. *Successful Publishing in Scholarly Journals*. Survival Skills for Scholars 11. Thousand Oaks, CA: SAGE, 1994.

Whicker, Marcia Lynn et al. *Getting Tenure*. Survival Skills for Scholars 8. Thousand Oaks, CA: SAGE, 1993.

Technology and Teaching

This bibliography is meant to encourage not only the use of new techniques but also an examination of their pedagogical and administrative advantages and disadvantages.

Althauser, Robert. "Collaborative Learning Via Study Groups and the Electronic Classroom." In *Collaborative Learning: Sourcebook for Collaborative Learning in the Arts and Sciences at Indiana University*. Edited by Sharon J. Hamilton and Edmund J. Hansen. Educational Resources Information Center: ERIC Document Reproduction Service (EDRS), 1992.

Breivik, Patricia S. *Student Learning in the Information Age*. American Council on Education Series on Higher Education. Phoenix, AZ: Oryx Press, 1998.

Chism, Nancy Van Note. "Handbook for Instructors on the Use of Electronic Class Discussion."[http://www.osu.edu/education/ftad/Publications/elecdisc/pages/home.htm __http://www.osu.edu/education/ftad/Publications/elecdisc/pages/home.htm_]

Coleman, Flick. "The Impact of the New Technologies on Education." *Wellesley Magazine* (Summer 1997): 12–15, 46–48.

Dyrli, Odvard Egil. "Teaching Effectively with Telecommunications." *Technology and Learning* 16, no. 5 (Feb 1996): 56ff.

Farber, Evan Ira et al. *Teaching and Technology: The Impact of Unlimited Information Access on Classroom Teaching*. Ann Arbor, Pierian Press, 1991.

Hilligoss, Susan and Cynthia L. Selfe, eds. *Literacy and Computers: The Complications of Teaching and Learning with Technology*. New York: Modern Language Association of America, 1994.

Holdstein, Deborah H. "Review: Technology, Utility, and Amnesia." *College English* 57, no. 5 (Sept 1995): 587–98.

Katz, Richard N. et al. *Dancing with the Devil: Information Technology and the New Competition in Higher Education*. San Francisco: Jossey-Bass, 1999.

Keating, Anne B. and Joseph Hargitai. *The Wired Professor: A Guide to Incorporating the World Wide Web in College Instruction*. New York and London: New York University Press, 1999.

Moulakis, Athanasios. "Beyond Utility: Liberal Education for a Technological Age." *Liberal Education 81*, no. 3 (Summer 1995): 28–35.

Oblinger, Diana G., and Sean C. Rush, eds. *The Learning Revolution: The Challenge of Information Technology in the Academy*. Bolton, MA: Anker, 1997.

Perkins, David N. et al. *Software Goes to School: Teaching for Understanding with New Technologies*. New York and Oxford: Oxford University Press, 1995.

Sharpless, Daniel R. "Collaborative Learning in an Electronic Classroom." In *Collaborative Learning*. Edited by Hamilton and Hansen. EDRS, 1992.

Lecturing

Andrews, Patricia Hayes. "Improving Lecturing Skills: Some Insights from Speech Communication." Teaching and Learning at Indiana University Series. Educational Resources Information Center: ERIC Document Reproduction Service (EDRS), 1989.

Bennett, Simon J. et al. "A Rapid Means of Student Evaluation of Lecturing Performance in Higher Education." *Assessment and Evaluation in Higher Education* 20, 2 (Aug 1995): 191–202.

Blum, Debra E. "For Academic Celebrities, the Lecture Circuit Can Be Hectic, Time-Consuming, and Sometimes Lucrative." *Chronicle of Higher Education* 37, no. 21 (Feb 6, 1991): A15.

Bonwell, Charles C. and James A. Eison. *Active Learning: Creating Excitement in the Classroom.* ASHE-ERIC Higher Education Report, no. 1. Washington, D.C.: George Washington University, 1991, pp. 7–21.

Brookfield, Stephen D. "Lecturing Creatively." *The Skillful Teacher: On Technique, Trust, and Responsiveness in the Classroom.* San Francisco: Jossey-Bass, 1990. 71–87.

Brown, George and Madeleine Atkins. "The Skills of Lecturing." *Effective Teaching in Higher Education.* London and New York: Methuen, 1988, pp. 19–49.

Bunnett, Joseph F. "Techniques for Spoiling Your Own Scientific Talk." *Journal of Chemical Education* 72, no. 12 (Dec 1995): 1119.

Burlbaw, Lynn Matthew. "Add a Teacher-Led Stimulation to Your Lecturing Techniques." *Social Studies* 82, 1 (Jan-Feb 1991): 30–31.

Burnett, Michael. "How to Be Demonstrably Entertaining: Techniques in Lecturing." *New Scientist* 128, no. 1742 (Nov 10, 1990): 58.
Cavanagh, Michael E. "Make Effective Speeches." *Personnel Journal* 67, no. 3 (March 1988): 51ff.

Davis, Barbara Gross. *Tools for Teaching.* San Francisco: Jossey-Bass, 1993, pp. 99–125.

Derek Bok Center for Teaching and Learning, Harvard University. "Tips for Teachers: Twenty Ways to Make Lectures More Participatory." Cambridge, MA: Derek Bok Center for Teaching and Learning, 1992. [http://www.fas.harvard.edu/~bok_cen]

Diamond, Robert M. *Designing and Assessing Courses and Curricula: A Practical Guide.* Revised ed. San Francisco: Jossey-Bass, 1998.

Dubrow, Heather and James Wilkinson. "The Theory and Practice of Lectures." In *The Art and Craft of Teaching*. Edited by Margaret M. Gullette. Cambridge, MA: Harvard University Press, 1984, pp. 25–37.

Eble, Kenneth A. *The Craft of Teaching*, 2d ed. San Francisco: Jossey-Bass, 1988, pp. 68–82.

Enerson, Diane, ed. *Teaching at Chicago: A Collection of Readings and Practical Advice for Beginning Teachers*. Chicago: University of Chicago Press, 1990.

George, Babu. "Will They Ever Learn? (Mistakes Speakers Usually Make)." *Chemtech* 19, no. 1 (Jan 1989).

Groves, Gerald. "The Lecture-Tutorial Composition Class: Everybody Wins." *Education* 108, no. 2 (Winter 1987): 217ff.

Gullette, Margaret M. "Leading Discussion in a Lecture Course: Some Maxims and an Exhortation." In *Teaching and the Case Method*. 3d ed. Edited by Louis B. Barnes, C. Roland Christensen and Abby J. Hansen. Boston: Harvard Business School Press, 1994, pp. 312–318.

Isaacs, Geoff. "Lecture Note-Taking, Learning and Recall." *Medical Teacher* 11, no. 304 (1989): 295–302.

——— "Lecturing Practices and Note-taking Purposes." *Studies in Higher Education* 19, no. 2 (1994): 203–16.

Jackson, M.W. "Less Lecturing, More Learning." *Studies in Higher Education* 14, 1 (1989): 55–68.

Jeffery, Gary H. "Seven Tips for Successful Classroom Speakers." *Instructor* 98, no. 4 (Nov-Dec 1988): 43.

Kiechel, Walter. "How to Give a Speech." *Fortune* 115 (June 8, 1987): 179ff.

Kuzbik, John. *Can We Talk? Effective Lecturing in the Classroom*. Instructional Strategies Series, no. 9. Educational Resources Information Center: ERIC Document Reproduction Service (EDRS), 1992.

McKeachie, Wilbert. *Teaching Tips: Strategies, Research and Theory for College and University Teachers*. Lexington, MA: D.C. Heath, 1994, pp. 53–70.

Meltzer, David E. "Promoting Interactivity in Physics Lecture Classes." *The Physics Teacher* 34, no. 2 (Feb 1996): 72ff.

Mosteller, Frederick. "The 'Muddiest Point in the Lecture' as a Feedback Device." *On Teaching and Learning: The Journal of the Harvard Danforth Center* (April 1989): 10–21.

Murray, Royce W. "Faraday's Advice to the Lecturer." *Analytical Chemistry* 64, no. 3 (Feb 1, 1992); 131.

Pope, Elizabeth, et al. *Public Speaking*. Cambridge, MA: Harvard-Radcliffe Speech Center, 1997.

Rigden, John S. "The Lost Art of Oratory." *Chemtech* 21, no. 9 (Sept 1991).

Schonwetter, Dieter J. "Attributes of Effective Lecturing in the College Classroom." *Canadian Journal of Higher Education* 23, 2 (1993): 1–18.

"Tips for Teachers: Twenty Ways to Make Lectures More Participatory." Cambridge, MA: Derek Bok Center for Teaching and Learning, 1992.

Weaver, R.L. Effective Lecture Techniques: Alternatives to Boredom." *New Direction in Teaching*, 7 (Winter 1982): 31–39.

Weimer, Maryellen, ed. *Teaching Large Classes Well*. San Francisco and London: Jossey-Bass, 1987.

Weimer, Maryellen and Rose Ann Neff, eds. *Teaching College: Collected Readings for the New Instructor*. Madison, WI: Atwood, 1998, 59–74.

CONTRIBUTORS

Todd Bodner is a doctoral student of social psychology at Harvard University. He has taught quantitative methods courses in a variety of academic disciplines including psychology, sociology, business administration, and statistics. His quantitative research interests include investigating the implications of taking multiple observations from each research subject on the interpretation of research results. His psychological research involves the study of barriers to flexible thought and behavior in educational and corporate contexts and how those barriers can be overcome.

James R. Dawes is a Junior Fellow at Harvard University's Society of Fellows. He has been a teaching fellow in courses on 19th- and 20th-century American prose and poetry. He is currently working on the representation of cultural trauma, war, and morality.

Anne E. Fernald is an assistant professor of English at Purdue University. After receiving her Ph.D. in English Literature from Yale University, she taught in the Expository Writing Program and in the Program on History and Literature at Harvard University. Her research focuses on modernism's relation to literary history. She has published on Virginia Woolf and is a contributing writer for the *Boston Book Review*.

Rebecca Jackman recently received her Ph.D. in Physical Chemistry from Harvard University. Her research involved the use of self-assembled monolayers for the fabrication of three-dimensional microstructures and she published several articles in this area. While at Harvard she was a teaching fellow and teaching consultant in chemistry for the Derek Bok Center and worked with non-native English speakers to refine their teaching skills. She is currently a post-doctoral fellow at the Massachusetts Institute of Technology.

Jennifer Kotilaine received her Ph.D in Music at Harvard University. Her dissertation examined the use of folk music as a symbol of national identity in post-Soviet Lithuania. She has taught both at Harvard and at Oberlin Conservatory, covering a wide variety of musical subjects from Gregorian chant to jazz, and 19th- century symphonies to African Music.

Jeffrey Marinacci received his M.A. in Sociology from Harvard University. His classroom experience includes undergraduate theory courses as well as graduate teacher-training seminars.

Sujay Rao is a Ph.D. candidate in Latin American History at Harvard University. He has taught undergraduates in History and Social Studies at Harvard University. He is currently researching the evolution of provincial and national governments in Argentina following independence.

Judith Richardson is a Ph.D. candidate in the History of American Civilization Program at Harvard University, and holds masters degrees in English from Harvard and in American Civilization from New York University. Having taught in the History and English departments at Harvard, she has recently been appointed a teaching fellow in the History and Literature program. She is currently researching haunted landscapes of the Hudson Valley.

Eric Towne received his B.A. in mathematics from Harvard University. He has been a Teaching Assistant in the Harvard Math Department for five years, where he is teaching calculus and studying the problem of squaring the wheel. He has also worked in investment banking at Goldman, Sachs & Co.

Kerry Walk teaches in the Expository Writing Program at Harvard College and is Assistant Director of the Harvard Writing Project. She received her Ph.D. in English from the University of California, Berkeley, where she taught composition for several years. A professional writing consultant with clients nation-wide, she lived for three years in Dunster House, one of Harvard's undergraduate residential colleges, as Resident Tutor in Academic Writing.

Leigh Weiss is a post-doctoral research fellow at the Harvard Business School. She received her PhD from Harvard University in Sociology, where she also received M.A. and B.A. degrees. Her research focuses on the social dimensions of knowledge management in knowledge-intensive organizations. She has worked at Goldman Sachs in London and as a consultant to several international businesses. She has taught undergraduates at Harvard, MBAs at the Harvard Business School and managers in private sector companies.

INDEX

A

academic demands, 37–38
"accidental hit," 90
accountability, student, 47
acids, strength of, 10
African music course, 23–26
Agnew, Eleanor, 76, 98n.6
algorithmic problem-solving, 3
Applied Imagination, 28
applying knowledge, xiv
art history seminar, 49, 50, 52, 54
Art and Craft of Teaching, The, 77
authority
    challenge to teacher's, 23–24
    in classroom, 43
    student, 25–26
    sharing of, 26
axtase, musical instrument, 23

B

"back-of-the-envelope" calculations, 6
Baker, Richard L., 87, 91, 98nn.2, 5
Baloche, L., 94n.9
barn raising, 27, 29–30
beliefs, intellectual, 58
big picture approach, 81–82, 85
blackboards, use of, 46–47
Bodner, Todd, xv, 81, 123
body language, 46
boiling point, definition of, 7
"boxing match," 30
Bonwell, C.C., 94n.1, 95n.1
brainstorming, 27, 28–29, 94n.4
Bransford, John D., 98n.1
bridge-speech, 43, 44–45
Bushey, Barbara, 95–96n.7

C

Chase, William G., 98n.1
chemistry instruction, teaching strategies,
    3–4
closure, 47–48
collaboration, barn raising, 30
collaborative learning, xiv
    barn raising, 29–30
    barriers to, 27
    brainstorming, 28–29
    in mathematics classes, 21
    in musicology, 26
    point/counterpoint arguing, 30–31
    reference sources for, 107–109
    scenario visioning, 33–34
    techniques for, 27–34
collaborative investigation, xiv, 53–54
collaborative problem-solving
    math-science, 13
    teacher-student, 39–40
collaborative restatement, bridge-speech,
    44–45
college teaching, bibliographical overviews,
    99
comments. *See* written comments
common goals, seminars, 49, 51–52
communication, reference sources for, 112–
    114
compartmentalization, of information, 6
conceptual learning
    chemistry, 3–4, 5, 7–8, 10
    mathematics, 13
connections
    chemistry course, 6–7
    statistics course, 82–83
content, control of, 49, 52–53

contextual relativism, 58
creativity
    barn raising, 30
    math and science courses, 13, 19–20
critical thinking, 13
cultural diversity, 23–26

D

Dawes, James, xiv, 43, 123
democracy, in classroom, 45–46
demonstrations, chemistry courses, 7–8
Derek Bok Center for Teaching and
    Learning, xiii
deroutinization, 43, 46–47
discussion groups, conceptual
    considerations, 49, 53–54
discussions
    agenda formulation, 52
    common goals, 51–52
    failures of, 37
    ground rules for, 51, 53
    group dynamics, 50–51
    limitations of, 20–21
    math and science courses, 14–17
    monitoring of, 52, 53
    principles of, 49
    process/content, 49–50, 53–54
    reference sources for, 105–106
    techniques of, 43–48
diversity, cultural, 23–26,
    reference sources for, 112–114
draft workshops, 71–72
drafting, writing process, 66–67
Drum Gahu patterns, 23, 25
dualistic thinking, 58

E

ego, 83–84
Eison, J. A., 94n.1, 95n.1
enthusiasm, student-teacher conferences,
    87
equations
    chemistry courses, 3, 4, 6–7
    role of, 5

equilibrium constant, 5
estimations, chemistry course, 6
ethical excellence, modeling, 87, 90
ethnomusicological research, 25–26
evaluations, and grading, 76–77
Evans, Kathryn, 89–90, 98n.3
Expository Writing course, 65, 87
extra help, student-teacher conferences, 87,
    88–90
extrinsic motivation, 58–59, 60

F

feedback, xiv–xv
    comments on student work, 77–78
    reference sources for, 110–111
    writing groups, 67, 68, 69
    written assignments, 58–61
Fernald, Anne, xv, 123
focus question, scenario visioning, 32
Freud, Sigmund, 81, 83–84

G

gankogui, musical instrument, 23
gender inequality, 28
Gere, Anne Ruggles, 67–68, 96–97nn.2, 4
Gibbs free energy, change in, 5
"Good Talk about Good Teaching," 90
Gordon, Harvey, 96n.1
grading, xv
    chemistry courses, 4
    correcting misconceptions, 84
    criteria for, 76, 77
    grade inflation, 75–76, 79
    opposition to, 76
    history course, 75
    problem sets, 85
    reference sources for, 110–111
    statistics course, 84, 85
    value of, 76–77
ground rules, discussion groups, 51, 53
group conferences, writing groups, 71
group discussions, xiv, 49, 53–54
group dynamics, 49, 50–51
Guzzio, Tracie Church, 98n.10

H

Harvard Magazine, 75, 76
"hidden agenda," 51
higher level thinking, 57–58

I

id, 83–84
independent thinking, math and science courses, 13
individualism
    contrasted with brainstorming, 29
    limitations of, 27
informant-of-the-week, 25–26
inquisitorial questions, 45
intellectual development, 58
intrinsic motivation, 58–59
intuition, math and science courses, 13
invitational questions, 45

J

Jackman, Rebecca, xiv, 3, 123
Jedrey, Christopher M., 77, 98nn.7, 9
job enrichment, barn raising, 29–30
Johnson, Marcia K., 98n.1
justifications, chemistry course, 6

K

kaganu, musical instrument, 23
Kahn, M., 94nn.6, 7
kidi, musical instrument, 23
kinetics, chemistry courses, 8
Kline, Nancy, 97n.6
knowledge sharing, 27–34
    barriers to, 27, 33
    benefits of, 27, 33–34
    business environment, 27, 33
    musicology, 26
    scenario visioning, 33
    students', 27, 33–34
    techniques of, 27, 33–34
Kotilaine, Jennifer, xiv, 23, 124

L

Lambert, Craig, 75, 97n.1
Larson, Laura, 98n.10

Latin American history course, 58
lectures, mathematics, 13, 14
lecturing, reference sources for, 119–121
Light, Richard, 57, 95n.2, 96n.9
linear functions, mathematics courses, 17, 18
Locke, David, 93n.1
Lowman, Joseph, 94–95n.1, 95n.5
Lucas, Ann F., 95n.1

M

Marinacci, Jeffrey, xiv, 37, 124
McKeachie, Wilbert J., 94–95n.1
"meaningful work," 30
"mediated intimacy," 87
memory, 7, 81–82
memorization, 5
mentor, teacher as, 90
metaphors, use of, 89, 90
McCormick, D., 94nn.6, 7
Michelangelo, 81
"mini-lecture," 47–48
"mirroring," 59
modeling, xiv, 53
    importance of, xiv, 91
    in writing groups, 71
motivation, student, 4, 10, 11, 13, 20–21, 27 57, 58–61, 65, 87–88
    fear, 75
    grades, 75
    reference sources for, 102–104
motivation, teacher, 4, 10, 11, 76–77, 87
    reference sources for, 102–104
multiple explanations, 89

N

names, memorizing students', 47
Nature, 82
Nimmer, James G., 97n.5

O

office space, 91
Osborn, A. F., 28, 29, 94nn.3,5

P

Palmer, Parker, 90
parabola, 19
parallels, chemistry course, 6–7
Patil, Parimal, 97n.3
pedagogical issues, cross-disciplinary, xiii
peer critique, 67–69
    reader response sheet, 70–71
Perry, William G., 95n.4
physical science, teaching strategies, 3–4
Placier, Margaret, 97n.4
planning, writing process, 66–67
"plug-and-chug problem-solving," 4–6
point-counterpoint argument, 27, 30–31
polynomials, evaluation of, 17–19
power, evacuation of, 43, 45–46
predictability, student-teacher conferences, 88
problem-solving
    brainstorming, 28
    chemistry courses, 3–4, 6
    math and science courses, 13
    "plug-and-chug approach," 4–6
    scenario visioning, 32–33
process, control of, 49, 52–53
professional concerns, 115–116
professors, pressure on, 37–38
    reference sources for, 115–116
psychic forces, conflict among, 81, 83–84

Q

quantitative courses, 81
questions
    chemistry course, 10
    focus, 32
    inquisitorial, 45
    invitational, 45
    mathematics courses, 14–16, 17, 18
    and restatements, 44–45
    reader response sheet, 70–71

R

Rao, Sujay, xiv, 57, 124
rate determining step (RDS), chemistry courses, 8–9

reader response sheet, 70–71
recognition
    grading, 79
    ritualization of, 43, 47–48
reflection, writing groups, 68
restatement, 44–45, 88–89
revision, in writing process, 66–67, 69–70
Richardson, Judith, xiv, 75, 124
rituals, student-teacher conferences, 87–88
Rodburg, Maxine, 97n.6

S

Sarton, May, 87
scenario visioning, 27, 32–33
Schoemaker, P., 94n.8
Science, 82
self-critique, writing groups, 65
self-evaluation, student, 78–79
Senior Teaching Fellows' Program, xiii
slope, 18, 19
small-group exercises, 44
Small Room, The, 87
sogo, musical instrument, 23
Sommers, Nancy, 69–70, 96n.3, 97n.5
spatial arrangements, 46
statistics course, 82–83
student motivation, reference sources for, 102–104
student presentations, bridge-speech, 45
student-teacher interactions
    conferences, xv, 87–91
    joint exploration of ideas, xiv, 52, 90–91
    physical setting, 91
students
    ability levels, 8, 17, 20
    blaming of, 38
    as junior colleagues, 52, 53
    learning styles, 3
    phases of intellectual development, 58, 95n.4
    procrastination of, 66–67
    self-evaluation, 78–79
    short term goals, 4

superego, 83–84
surface tension, demonstration of, 8

T-U
Taylor approximations, mathematics
    courses, 14
teacher motivation, 4, 10, 11, 76–77, 87
    reference sources for,102–104
teaching
    ineffective, 37–40
    professional concerns bibliography,
        115–116
    recommended techniques, 100–101
    technology and, 117–118
Towne, Eric, xiv, 13, 124
triangulation, student-teacher conferences,
    89
university teaching, bibliographical
    overviews, 99

V
"voice," 49
voices, democratization of, 45–46

W-Y-Z
Walk, Kerry, xiv, 65, 98, 124
Weimer, Maryellen, 94–95n.1
Weiss, Leigh, xiv, 125
Western tradition, musical bias, 24–25
What Maisie Knew, 90
Williams, John A., 93n.2
Winkelmes, Mary-Ann, 49, 125
writing assignments
    drafts, 65–68, 71–72, 87
    feedback on, 58–61
    revisions,65–67, 87–88
    weekly/regular, 57–58
writing groups, 65, 67–68, 69–71, 72
    objections to, 68–69
writing process, 66
writing skills, teaching of, 65–66
written comments, 58–62
    grading, 77–78
    statistics course, 84–85
    storage of, 85
y-intercept, 18, 19
Zulu isikhunzi music, 26

ABOUT THE AUTHORS

MARY-ANN WINKELMES is Associate Director at the Derek Bok Center for Teaching and Learning at Harvard University and teaches the history of Italian Renaissance art and architecture at Harvard University Extension School. She received her Ph.D. in the history of art and architecture from Harvard University and her M.A. in the history of art from Yale University. She has published on Benedictine church design and decoration, acoustics and religious architecture, nuns as patrons of art and architecture in Renaissance Italy, and college teaching.

JAMES WILKINSON is Director of the Derek Bok Center for Teaching and Learning at Harvard University. He received his Ph.D. in European history from Harvard University and has published widely on both pedagogy and European intellectual history in professional journals. In addition, he is author of *The Intellectual Resistance in Europe* and co-author of *Contemporary Europe: A History.*